# A2 English Language & Literature

# UNIT 4

## AQA

Specification B

## Module 4: Text Transformation

John Shuttleworth

Philip Allan Updates
Market Place
Deddington
Oxfordshire
OX15 0SE

*Orders*
Bookpoint Ltd, 130 Milton Park, Abingdon, Oxfordshire, OX14 4SB
tel: (44) 01235 827720
fax: (44) 01235 400454
e-mail: uk.orders@bookpoint.co.uk
Lines are open 9.00 a.m.–5.00 p.m., Monday to Saturday, with a 24-hour message answering service. You can also order through our website: www.philipallan.co.uk

© Philip Allan Updates 2006

ISBN-13: 978-1-84489-550-2
ISBN-10: 1-84489-550-5

This guide has been written specifically to support students preparing for AQA Specification B English Language and Literature Unit 4 coursework. The content has been neither approved nor endorsed by AQA and remains the sole responsibility of the author.

Printed by MPG Books, Bodmin

*Environmental information*
The paper on which this title is printed is sourced from managed, sustainable forests.

# Contents

## Introduction

■ ■ ■

## Content Guidance

■ ■ ■

## Transformations and Commentaries

# Introduction

## About this guide

This unit guide deals with the AQA Specification B A2 English Language and Literature **Module 4: Text Transformation**, and will help you to prepare, write and submit a successful folder of coursework for moderation. There are three sections:

- **Introduction** — this explains exactly what you are required to do for the module, and outlines how text transformations build on the skills you have learnt and practised in other parts of the course. It outlines how your teacher and moderator will assess your work, and suggests how to present a successful folder.
- **Content Guidance** — this provides a guide to choosing suitable texts for transformation and suggests how such texts might be transformed. It also considers what to include in a successful commentary and some of the terminology you might use.
- **Transformations and commentaries** — this includes the transformations and commentaries submitted by three candidates, awarded A, C and D grades. Moderator comments, preceded by the icon 𝓜, point out the strengths and weaknesses of each candidate.

In this module, you have to choose a literary work of any genre, written in or translated into English. Then, using the skills and knowledge you have acquired and practised in your work for AS, you must transform your chosen work into a different genre or sub-genre. This new genre does not have to be a literary one, but you must be able to demonstrate that there are links and interplay between your chosen source text and your transformation. In addition, you must submit a commentary on your work, in which you reflect and comment on the transformation that you have produced.

You must keep the length of the transformation and commentary within certain word count limits, as this is one of the criteria by which your teacher and moderator will assess your folder. The transformation should be between 1,500 and 2,500 words. The commentary should be between 1,500 and 2,000 words.

If you wish, you may write two shorter transformations (with the same overall word limit) based on the same source text, or two shorter transformations based on two different source texts. If you choose a long source text (e.g. a Jane Austen or Charles Dickens novel) you are not expected to base your transformation on the entire text. You are allowed to select suitable sections from such works.

Most students find text transformation enjoyable and rewarding. Here are some comments from students who have already completed the course:

- 'I had a lot of fun as well as learning a great deal during my text transformation work.'
- 'It was the part of the course that I enjoyed the most.'
- 'I just wonder what Jane Austen would have made of my chav version of *Pride and Prejudice*!'

Teachers and moderators seem to enjoy it as well. This is what one moderator had to say: 'It's a pleasure to read work from so many talented candidates. It's rare for me actually to look forward to receiving folders from centres. With text transformation, I certainly do!'

## How the text transformation links with the AS course

Your work for AS has given you a firm foundation for Module 4: Text Transformation. You have already prepared and submitted a folder of coursework for Module 3: Production of Texts, in which you had to write texts for particular audiences and purposes, using appropriate language in order to communicate successfully with your chosen audience. It is just as important to demonstrate these skills in your text transformation.

Module 3 also showed you how important it is to use an appropriate genre for your chosen audience and purpose and to employ the stylistic conventions associated with that particular genre. You may, for example, have chosen to write a newspaper article, a short story or a script for a radio documentary and will have had to ensure that what you produced for your folder was in the appropriate style. Again, you will be using such skills when you produce your text transformation.

Your work for AS also introduced you to a number of literary texts and genres, which will be useful when planning your text transformation. For example, you studied a range of poems from your Anthology during Module 1: Introduction to Language and Literature Study, and you have read two novels for Module 2: The Changing Language of Literature.

## How your folder is assessed

Your submitted folder is marked according to **assessment objectives**. These are the criteria that the examination board uses when assessing your work. Teachers and moderators have to judge the skills, knowledge and understanding you show in the transformation and commentary in the light of these assessment objectives. For this module, they are:

| AO1 | Communicate clearly the knowledge, understanding and insights gained from the combination of literary and linguistic study, using appropriate terminology and accurate written expression. |
|---|---|
| AO4 | Show understanding of the ways contextual variation and choices of form, style and vocabulary shape the meaning of texts. |
| AO5 | Identify and consider the ways attitudes and values are created and conveyed in speech and writing. |
| AO6 | Demonstrate expertise and accuracy in writing for a variety of specific purposes and audiences, drawing on knowledge of literary texts and features of language to explain and comment on the choices made. |

In practice, the assessment objectives are applied to the transformation and commentary as outlined below.

## The transformation

For the transformation, there are four main criteria against which your work will be judged: use of source text, control of genre, audience and quality of written English.

### Use of source text

The purpose of this unit is to transform a literary source text. Your submission will therefore be judged on how much understanding of the original text your transformation demonstrates and how much interplay there is between the original and new text. Your teacher and moderator will be looking at whether your transformation provides interesting new insights and perspectives on the source text and, naturally enough, whether it is enjoyable to read.

### Control of genre

Your transformation should be written in a medium that is significantly different from the genre of your source text. Your folder will therefore be assessed on how well you have shown that you understand and have used the conventions associated with your chosen new genre and whether you have sustained your use of these conventions throughout your work.

### Audience

You should have a particular audience in mind when writing your transformation. Your work will therefore be judged on how appealing and suitable it is for this audience.

### Quality of written English

Your teacher and moderator will assess your spelling, punctuation, grammar and syntax — you should aim to demonstrate a high level of technical accuracy in English.

## The commentary

There are three main criteria against which your commentary is judged: comments on the discourses of both texts, comments on changes and comments on language.

### Comments on discourses of both texts

The discourse of a text includes its genre, purpose, audience, structure and context. Your ability to demonstrate an understanding of these topics in your source text and its transformation will be examined, so you must make comments on these essential and significant aspects of the transformation.

### Comments on changes

Your work will be assessed on how clearly and effectively you comment on both the purpose and effect of the changes you have made from the source text to the new text.

### Comments on language

The intended audience and purpose of your new text should have a significant impact on your choice of language. Your teacher and moderator will assess your commentary on the level of understanding you have shown when writing about the language choices and changes you have made. If you are using technical terminology to describe your choices, they will look to see if you have used it accurately.

The word limit for the commentary has already been mentioned. This word limit means that you will not be able to comment on every aspect of your transformation. You will therefore also be assessed on how perceptive and central your comments are to your work.

## How marks are awarded

There are 30 marks available for the transformation and 30 for the commentary.

When you have completed a paper in a written, end-of-unit examination, it is sent to an external examiner, who assesses your script and awards it a mark. You will not be aware of this mark until you receive your results a few weeks later. However, the process is different for a coursework unit such as Text Transformation, because your teacher marks your work, not an external examiner. When you submit your final folder to your teacher, he/she will assess it and award it a mark according to the criteria outlined above. Your teacher will then discuss your work with colleagues in your school/college and will agree on a final mark for your transformation and commentary to submit to the examination board.

In the next stage of the marking process, a moderator (appointed by the examination board) rereads a small sample of the folders from your school/college to see if your teachers have awarded accurate marks in line with ones awarded by teachers in other centres for similar work. If the moderator agrees with the marks for this sample of folders, then all the marks for candidates from your centre are accepted by the examination board. If there is disagreement between the moderator and the centre, the mark awarded by the moderator will be the one you are given.

In any case, you will probably have a good idea of the standard you have achieved before all these stages in the marking process take place. Before you hand in your coursework, you will have worked on it for a number of weeks, drafting and redrafting, polishing and honing it in the light of advice from your teacher, until both of you are satisfied that this is the best work you can produce.

## The transformation

This section outlines what is acceptable and unacceptable as a transformation, and indicates briefly some of the skills you will require.

In your transformation:
- there must be a significant difference between the genre of the source text and the genre of the new text
- some new and enlightening insight or perspective on the source text must be gained from reading your new text

To gain a high mark in your transformation, you must:

- choose a source text that is recognised as being from a *literary* genre or sub-genre
- choose a source text that will enable you to transform it in some *significant* way
- ensure that there are *links* between the two texts
- accept the need for planning, *drafting* and redrafting to ensure that your final version is the best you can produce

There are two types of text transformation: **adaptation** and **transformation**.

In the first, a source text is *adapted* or reworked into another medium. You will be familiar with the notion of **adaptation** of classic novels for film, television and radio programmes, e.g. *Pride and Prejudice*. The adapter took the characters, plot and settings of Jane Austen's novel and adapted them for the conventions of the new medium — film costume drama. Homer's *Odyssey* was also adapted recently for a radio drama, in which all the opportunities presented by radio were used to bring Homer's stories vividly to life. Such adaptations would have been entirely acceptable as text transformations.

In the second, a source text undergoes significant *transformation* into another genre, while still retaining identifiable links with the original text. A **transformation** takes a theme, character or plot aspect from a source text and changes and re-presents it from a different point of view, with a different emphasis or for a different audience. There must be a clearly discernible link between your source text and your transformation. For example, you might choose Christopher Marlowe's play *Dr Faustus* as your source text and transform this story of a man who makes a pact with the devil. There are many possibilities for transformation in this text — updating the setting and characters, reworking the theme of temptation and ultimate disappointment, writing it as a science-fiction story etc. — but keep in mind that there must be some interplay between the two texts and that the transformation must throw new light or insight on the original.

You must *not* use your source text merely as a springboard into a piece of creative or original writing that has no connection with the source text. Springboarding is discussed further in the Content Guidance section on p. 22.

There is, of course, some degree of overlap between the two types of transformation. Baz Luhrmann's film version of Shakespeare's *Romeo and Juliet* is a case in point. Luhrmann *adapted* the original play to a film script, thus changing the medium. At the same time, he transformed the play by updating its setting to the west coast of the USA and by changing some of the language and emphases of the original text. The final product is not simply a filmed presentation of a stage play.

There is no advantage in choosing either type of transformation. They are assessed in exactly the same way and moderators do not favour one over the other.

## The commentary

The commentary is worth exactly the same number of marks as the transformation, so you should put just as much effort into this part of your folder.

The best way to think about a commentary is to see it as a writer reflecting on the processes he/she went through to arrive at the final published text. You, of course, are the writer in question. It can also be helpful to consider other writers to be the audience for this commentary — this should focus your mind on what it is vital to comment on. When a moderator looks at your submitted folder, he/she will read your commentary before reading your transformation in order to see what your intentions were and to examine the significant decisions you made. He/she will also be looking to see if the claims you make in your commentary are borne out by what you have written in the transformation.

Your commentary should contain your thoughts and reflections on some or all of the following:
- the audience, genre, style and structure of your source text and new text
- links between the source and the transformation
- changes you have made between these texts and the reasons for these changes
- changes you have made between drafts of your new text
- the language of your new text

This list is not exhaustive and you can also comment on other aspects of your work.

## Drafting

There are few, if any, writers whose published work appears as it was initially written. This book is no exception. The idea that a writer sits down at his/her desk and waits for inspiration until the finished product flows from pen or keyboard is a myth. In reality, writing is planned, sketched out, drafted, written, edited and then rewritten several times before publication. In this way, the writer tries to ensure that the work the reader encounters is the finest that he/she can produce and that it is as well suited to its audience and purpose as possible.

Your work on the text transformation should undergo the same processes. Planning, drafting, editing and rewriting are essential. You should listen to the advice of teachers and other interested and qualified readers at all stages of your writing and act on this advice. Even famous and bestselling authors rely on their editors and often pay tribute to the help received from them. You should learn from their example. Do not be satisfied with your first attempt; be prepared to change, excise, restructure and rewrite, probably more than once. It will pay dividends.

## What your folder of work should contain

It is important that the folder you give to your teacher (and therefore, perhaps, to a moderator) is complete, well organised and neatly presented. There is no requirement for you to word process your submission, but most candidates choose to do so.

The best folders contain the following clearly labelled items in the order in which they appear:

- **The transformation** — this should be the final, definitive version of your work. It should contain no annotation by your teacher or any other form of marking.
- **The commentary** — again, this should be the final, definitive version of your work and should be free from any annotation or marking.
- **Drafts of the transformation** — you should include all of your drafts. There is no need to remove any comments, marks or suggestions from them.
- **Drafts of the commentary** — you are also likely to have drafted and redrafted your commentary. These, too, should be included together with any marks or annotations on them.
- **The source text** — if you (or your teacher) think that your source text is likely to be unfamiliar to your moderator, you should include a copy. If it is a substantial text such as a novel or long poem, you need not include the whole text, but only the section that is most relevant to your transformation.
- **Your style or genre model** — if you have chosen to write your transformation in imitation of what may be an unfamiliar style or genre, your moderator will find it helpful if you include an example of this genre or style. This should prevent him/her from misjudging your submission.

# Content
# Guidance

This section covers the important aspects of text transformation. You need to be familiar with these before you begin work on your transformation and its accompanying commentary.

Advice is given on how to choose an appropriate literary source text for your transformation. This is followed by an outline of the types of transformation that are acceptable for the unit together with advice on how to produce a successful piece of work. Tips are also given on types of transformation to avoid.

This section also considers the commentary, covering relevant topics to discuss, as well as comments that should be excluded.

# Choosing a source text

First, a reminder of what the specification says about choosing a text: '...candidates are required to take a literary work of any genre...in order to transform the original work into a different genre or sub-genre'. As with most specifications, this only provides you with the bare bones of what is required; there are many issues that you need to consider before deciding on the text (or texts) that you wish to transform.

The following paragraphs explore the issues surrounding your choice of text and help you decide on the best type for you.

## Class texts or individual texts

When selecting a source text, each member of your class may be allowed to decide upon their own text. However, your teacher may decide that it is better for all members of the class to transform the same text, or may opt to give the class a choice from two or three. The examination board does not favour either of these alternatives over the other, and your marks will not be affected by other members of your class transforming the same source material.

If, however, all members of one class are asked to transform the same source text into the same genre or medium, this may have an effect on the marks awarded. For example, not everyone is equally skilled in writing short stories, radio scripts or magazines articles. If possible, it is better for each candidate to choose to write in a genre that they enjoy and feel comfortable with.

The remainder of the advice in this section assumes that your teacher has given you the opportunity to choose your own text to transform. However, you should discuss your choice carefully with your teacher and listen to, and act upon, any advice that may be offered.

## Written texts

Occasionally, a student wants to use as a source text a fairy tale, a nursery rhyme, a myth (e.g. Theseus and the Minotaur) or a story from the Bible. While such choices are permitted, there *must* always be a written version of these stories available to your teacher and moderator. You *must not* base your transformation solely on an oral version or on your memory of the story. So, for example, if you choose to transform a fairy tale, you could use the version written by the Brothers Grimm or by Perrault and, of course, ensure that you use an English translation.

## Literary texts

The specification requires you to choose a *literary* text as your source. There are three main *genres* of literary text: drama, poetry and prose fiction. The latter includes both novels and short stories. The majority of successful transformations are based on texts from these main genres, so it is advisable that you do the same. There is no doubt about the acceptability of canonical, or mainstream, literary texts such as novels by Charlotte Brontë or Graham Greene, poems by Wilfred Owen or Carol Ann Duffy, and plays by William Shakespeare or Arthur Miller. There are, of course, many other lesser-known writers who would also be entirely acceptable.

These main literary genres can be divided into *sub-genres*, which conservative critics sometimes regard as less satisfactory than mainstream texts. Some of the sub-genres of prose fiction could be classified as detective fiction, science fiction or 'chick lit'. Poetry and drama can be similarly subdivided. You are free to choose such texts for your transformation, as the marks awarded are based solely on the quality of the transformation and its accompanying commentary. Remember, however, that the more challenging and substantial the source text, the more successful the transformation is likely to be.

However, some texts cannot be regarded as literary and you should not choose to transform them. Newspaper editorials, footballers' ghost written memoirs and cookery books are just three of the genres that the occasional student has tried to use and which were deemed unacceptable by the examination board. You must use a text from a literary genre or sub-genre.

Some genres of text are less easy to categorise as literary or non-literary. These can include diaries, autobiographies, memoirs. If you are drawn to this type of text as your source, it is vital that you consult your teacher before embarking on your transformation. Do not be one of those candidates whose work is marked harshly because of an unacceptable source text. Remember, it is safest to choose a mainstream literary text.

## Substantial texts

Even when a text can be regarded as belonging to a literary genre or sub-genre, it may not be advisable to use it as a source text for transformation. If the text does not have sufficient 'weight' in itself, it will be extremely difficult to transform successfully. For example, lyrics to a pop song are occasionally chosen as source texts. Leaving aside the issue of whether song lyrics can be regarded as literary, it is certainly true that most pop lyrics would not support a transformation that is substantial enough to gain marks in the top brackets. It is vital that you choose a source text that will enable you to reach the highest marks possible.

Other genres may be similarly tempting to use, but can be equally problematic. For example, it is tempting to use texts that you are very familiar with or have loved dearly, e.g. stories or poems written for children (including nursery rhymes). However, the danger remains: except in the hands of the most talented candidates, such texts do not provide enough substantial material for use as a base for transformation. The advice to choose a substantial text from one of the mainstream genres remains the best option for most candidates.

## GCSE texts

There can be a temptation to choose a text that you studied for GCSE. This is understandable, as you are likely to be familiar with these texts and hopefully you enjoyed them. However, you should resist this temptation as you may not come to them with a fresh perspective, and they may not be sufficiently challenging for text transformation at A-level. Teachers and moderators find that transformations based on GCSE texts are usually unambitious and tired, and do not allow candidates to access the highest marks. So, even if you loved texts such as *Of Mice and Men*, *An Inspector Calls* or *To Kill a Mockingbird* when you studied them for GCSE, you would now be better advised to choose another to transform.

## Combinations of texts

Most candidates base their transformation on one text, although some choose to use a combination of texts. For example, one candidate produced a transformation that included four of Shakespeare's female characters — Lady Macbeth, Juliet, Desdemona and Cleopatra — and another wrote a script for a documentary about *Big Brother* using two characters from Ibsen's *A Doll's House* and J. D. Salinger's *Catcher in the Rye*. Both of these transformations were very effective.

However, you will not impress the moderator any more by using a combination of texts than you will by producing a good transformation based on just one source text. One candidate thought that this was the case and wrote a transformation based on six texts — he achieved low marks because he was not able to handle the complexities involved.

## Clear links

When choosing a text to transform, remember that you must be able to create clearly demonstrable links and interplay between the source and the new text. If your transformation does not provide a new and enlightening perspective on your source text, then you have not written a text transformation.

## Test yourself

Below is a list of texts and their authors. Find out what you can about each text and decide whether you think it is suitable to be used as a source for transformation. All of these texts have been used by previous candidates, with varying degrees of success.

| | |
|---|---|
| 'Please Mrs Butler' | Allan Ahlberg |
| *Pride and Prejudice* | Jane Austen |
| *A Cream Cracker under the Settee* | Alan Bennett |
| *Scoring at Half Time* | George Best |
| 'David and Goliath' | from the Bible |

| | |
|---|---|
| 'The Sick Rose' | William Blake |
| *Noddy goes to Toytown* | Enid Blyton |
| 'Journey of the Magi' | T. S. Eliot |
| 'Mosh' | Eminem |
| *The Poisonwood Bible* | Barbara Kingsolver |
| 'When I'm Sixty Four' | Paul McCartney |
| 'The Highwayman' | Alfred Noyes |
| *The Republic* | Plato |
| *Mort* | Terry Pratchett |
| *Harry Potter and the Philosopher's Stone* | J. K. Rowling |
| *Educating Rita* | Willy Russell |
| *King Lear* | William Shakespeare |
| *Of Mice and Men* | John Steinbeck |
| *The Importance of Being Earnest* | Oscar Wilde |
| *A Streetcar Named Desire* | Tennessee Williams |

# The transformation

The Introduction outlined the two main ways of transforming a source text: *adaptation* and *transformation*. This section looks at these two methods in more detail.

## Adapting a source text

Changing your source text (or part of it) in order to present it in another medium is a popular way of approaching this unit. There are many examples for you to study in the professional media world. Novels are adapted for film (*Oliver Twist, Bridget Jones's Diary, Lord of the Rings*), for television serials (*The Woman in White, Barchester Towers*) and for radio (*Northanger Abbey, Tess of the d'Urbervilles*). Stage plays are turned into films (*The Madness of King George, Henry V*), and poems become radio plays (*Paradise Lost*, 'My Last Duchess').

If you decide to adapt your source text for a new medium then it is vital that you are aware of its conventions. For example, it is no use adapting your favourite novel or short story into a radio play or serial if you never listen to radio plays or serials. If you do not watch many films, it would be unwise to choose film as the new medium for your transformation. Nor is it merely a matter of listening to a few radio adaptations or watching a film version of a novel and thinking that this is all you need do. You must listen or watch with the purpose of understanding the methods and conventions of your chosen new medium so that you can use them in your own work.

Take radio drama as an example. When you listen to a radio play adapted from another medium, you need to ask questions such as:

- What is the dialogue doing? (e.g. moving the plot along, portraying character, establishing time and space)
- Has new dialogue been created? Why?
- How is one character differentiated from another in terms of speech?
- Does a character's speech remain consistent throughout?
- How often do the speakers change?
- How often does the speech change pace?
- How are scene changes managed?
- Does each scene have its own structure — tension, climax and resolution?
- Does the order of events remain the same?
- What sound effects and music are used? What are they used for?
- Has the adapter used a narrator?
- How have long stretches of narrative in the source text been adapted for radio?
- What, if anything, has been omitted from (or added to) the original text (e.g. characters)? Why?

A careful study of a number of radio dramas should provide you with answers to these questions and show you what the conventions of this medium are. Most importantly, such careful study should enable you to adapt your source text effectively and will provide material for your commentary.

The detailed preparation and research outlined above is essential, whatever medium and genre you choose, and must be carried out before you even start the first draft of your adaptation.

## Transforming a source text

Although there are many differences between adaptation and transformation, there are also many similarities, and you will need to go through the same processes for both types of text transformation:

- Choose a genre which you enjoy and are familiar with.
- Read carefully and purposefully as many examples of your chosen genre as you can.
- Study these examples to ascertain the conventions of the genre, and the appropriate language and style for your chosen audience.
- Use these conventions, language and style in your transformation.
- Never forget that there must be discernible links and imaginative interplay between the source and the transformation: the one must throw light on the other.

The following table lists ten examples of recent successful transformations submitted by candidates.

| Source text | Transformation |
|---|---|
| *Macbeth* (Shakespeare) | Short story set in the world of international finance |
| 'Porphyria's Lover' (Robert Browning) | Psychiatrist's report on the murderer |
| 'David and Goliath' (Old Testament) | Story of gang warfare set in modern-day Brixton |
| *A Streetcar Named Desire* (Tennessee Williams) | Soviet Socialist realistic novel of the 1930s |
| Selection of Wilfred Owen's poems | Hitchhiker's Guide to the First World War (written in the style of Douglas Adams) |
| *Twelfth Night* (Shakespeare) | Japanese graphic novel |
| *Lysistrata* (ancient Greek play by Aristophanes) | *News of the World* feature article about sex strikes |
| *The Bell Jar* (Sylvia Plath) | Collection of poetry |
| 'To His Coy Mistress' (Andrew Marvell) | Play set in modern-day Hull from the point of view of the woman (now a 17-year-old girl) |
| 'The Laboratory' (Robert Browning) | Chapter from a new Harry Potter novel |

# Types of transformation

It is impossible in this unit guide to list all the conventions of the many different genres that candidates choose. However, two of the most popular (if not always the most successful), namely short stories and newspaper articles, are examined below. Where they are unsuccessful it is often because the candidate has not read enough short stories or newspaper articles to properly understand their conventions.

## Short stories

Before writing your transformation short story, you must read as many good examples of the genre as you can and, as you read, ask yourself the following questions about them. Your answers to these questions should demonstrate to you how a short story is structured and organised.

- Who are the characters?
- How are they introduced and established?
- What is the main incident in or subject of the short story?
- What conflicts take place?
- How is the setting established?
- What makes a strong start to the story?
- Is there variety of pace within the story?
- From whose point of view is the story narrated?

- What use is made of dialogue or monologue?
- What does the ending accomplish?

In composing your short-story transformation, you have an advantage over short-story writers who have to start with a blank canvas. They have to invent everything, whereas you have your source text to begin with. Remember that your teacher and moderator will be looking to see how successful your transformation is as a short story, as well as whether it throws new light on the source text.

## Newspaper articles

As you read newspaper articles with a critical eye, focused on the conventions of the genre you will notice that they:
- have an arresting headline
- begin with the most interesting piece of information or a summary of the story
- move from the most newsworthy aspects of the story to the least as the article progresses
- focus early on the who, what, where, when, why and how of the story
- ensure that the reader is led clearly and simply from point to point
- caption any pictures clearly and that they are closely linked to the story

If you follow these conventions when you are writing your transformation newspaper article you will have every chance of producing an effective piece of work. It is not sufficient merely to make your piece look like an article in its layout and presentation; it must follow the conventions listed above.

Whatever genre you decide upon for your transformation, it is essential that you make yourself familiar with its conventions. This will ensure that you have gone some way to producing an effective new text.

## Literary and non-literary transformations

It is not always easy to decide whether a particular genre is either literary or non-literary as the distinction between the two can be somewhat blurred. For example, is a diary literary or non-literary? Does your opinion change when considering your diary or Samuel Pepys's? What about a pop song or lyric poem? How different are travel brochures and travel writing?

The mega-genres of poetry, prose fiction and drama are usually (though not always) recognised as literary, whereas some categories of writing are generally thought to be non-literary — police reports, classified advertisements, A-level essays. These distinctions are important to remember, as you must choose an appropriate source text to transform.

There are no such difficulties when it comes to choosing a text type (or genre) for the transformation itself — they are all acceptable. However, the majority of candidates choose from the recognised literary mega-genres or their associated sub-genres. These genres are not suitable for every candidate, and you may be happier and better served by avoiding them. Some non-literary genres are easier to replicate and adapt than the more mainstream literary ones. As always, if you are in doubt as to which is most suitable for you, consult your teacher.

The following table shows some examples of non-literary genres chosen by successful candidates for their transformations.

| Source text | Author | Genre | Transformed into |
| --- | --- | --- | --- |
| 'Eveline' | James Joyce | Short story | Newspaper article on domestic violence |
| Tom Brown's Schooldays | Thomas Hughes | Novel | E-mails home |
| The Bell Jar | Sylvia Plath | Novel | Psychiatric report |
| 1984 | George Orwell | Novel | Political speech |
| 'Ozymandias' | P. B. Shelley | Poem | Travel writing |
| 'Sir Gawain and the Green Knight' | Anon. poem | Medieval narrative | Article for a tabloid newspaper |
| Pride and Prejudice | Jane Austen | Novel | Handbook on etiquette |
| Romeo and Juliet | Shakespeare | Play | Text messages |
| Frankenstein | Mary Shelley | Novel | Victorian problem pages |
| A Streetcar Named Desire | Tennessee Williams | Play | Social worker's report |
| The Curious Incident of the Dog in the Night-Time | Mark Haddon | Novel | Radio documentary |

These are not the only non-literary genres that you can use for your transformation. You should choose your new genre because you are familiar with it, will enjoy transforming your source text into it and are certain that it will provide illuminating interplay between the two texts.

# Transformations to avoid

Some types of transformation do not allow candidates to demonstrate their abilities to best effect. You should avoid these options, however attractive they might at first seem.

## Genres that are too similar

When looking at a folder of work, moderators ask: 'Is there sufficient difference between the genre of the source text and that of the transformation?' They do this for a good reason — if the genres are too close together, then little or no transformation can take place.

Take, as an example, a student who chooses to turn a play script into a film script. Apart from the stage directions concerning the set and the lighting, the remainder of a play script is likely to be dialogue. A film script will be basically the same — there will be detailed information about setting, lighting, camera shots and angles, but the rest of the script will be dialogue for the actors. You need to look at only a few examples of published play and film scripts to see the similarities between the two. If the candidate wishes to keep his/her adaptation or transformation faithful to the original play text, there is little scope to change this dialogue apart from minor additions or deletions.

For the purposes of text transformation, plays adapted into films may be modernised, or their setting may be changed, as in Baz Luhrmann's version of *Romeo and Juliet*. However, when a candidate adapts a play script with the intention of staying as faithful as possible to the original, this is not a suitable text transformation — there will insufficient distinction between the two texts. The same argument applies to the transformation of a novel to a short story, or vice versa — there is too much similarity of genre to produce a successful text transformation without some other aspect of the text being changed.

Students who are tempted down this path almost invariably end up with low marks. To ensure success, you must choose a genre for your transformation that is sufficiently distinct from the genre of your source text.

## The diary syndrome

Have you ever kept a diary? Most people have probably kept a record of their daily activities at some time in their lives, although they are also likely to give up writing a diary after a short time. Even the most famous diarist of all — Samuel Pepys — wrote for only 9 of his 70 years.

Many candidates write text transformations in which their new text purports to have been written by a character in the source text. Teachers and moderators groan when they encounter, for instance, yet another example of Eva Smith's diary based on the character in J. B. Priestley's *An Inspector Calls*, or Lady Macbeth's from Shakespeare's play. Why? Because the majority of characters from literature are not the sort of people who would keep a diary.

There are other arguments against writing the diary of a character for your submission. First, diarists do not usually intend their diaries to be published, and they frequently use coded or unclear language. Second, because the intended audience for a diary is usually restricted to one reader, candidates often attempt to deal with this by using the outmoded and stilted concept of 'Dear Diary'. Finally, the time shifts and variation of pace and events in novels do not fit well into a daily diary entry — it is unconvincing to return to writing a diary after a gap of, say, 10 years.

To conclude, not many diaries make interesting reading for people who are not involved in the events described or do not know the people involved. *The Diary of Anne Frank* is a notable exception, as is *Bridget Jones's Diary* (although this is not really a diary). You should therefore resist the temptation to use the diary genre for your transformation, as it is rarely, if ever, successful.

## Springboarding

An essential feature of text transformation, as previously discussed, is that the new text should throw light on the source text. This new light is often referred to as 'insight', 'interplay' or 'perspective'. If no new insight is made, the new text will not constitute a text transformation, no matter how well-written or enjoyable it might be, and it will be marked down accordingly.

If you present a transformation with no discernible connection to the source text, then you have springboarded from the old text to the new. Some candidates produce transformations that focus only on the setting, a theme or a type of character from the source text without ensuring that there is a substantial link with the original text. Two examples from recent submissions will help to clarify the concept of 'springboarding'.

'The Rime of the Ancient Mariner' by Coleridge is a well-known poem, which tells the story of a doomed sea voyage. It contains many haunting descriptions of being stranded at sea on a ship full of dead and dying sailors. One transformation that claimed to be based on the poem was a short story set on board a ship, but the story had no links with the themes, atmosphere or characters of Coleridge's original. The candidate felt that his text was a transformation because the settings were similar. It wasn't.

*The Catcher in the Rye* by J. D. Salinger is a popular novel about adolescent angst, set in New York in the 1950s. The candidate who transformed this into a radio play about teenagers did not fulfil the requirements of the specification. She thought that it was sufficient to take the age of the characters from the novel, without making connection to the themes and ideas of Salinger's original work. It wasn't.

You must ensure that you, your teacher and the moderator can perceive the links between your two texts. You should use your commentary to clarify these links.

## Scripting the unscriptable

One of the most popular genres for the transformation is the radio script. However, there is a pitfall — that of writing a script (or part of a script) that would not, in reality, be scripted at all. Take, for example, the radio phone-in. This by its very nature cannot be scripted, because you cannot predict what the speaker will say. The same applies to a live interview. You can have no idea what the interviewee is going to say. However, some transformations do contain just this spontaneous speech and the result is that they become extremely artificial and unconvincing, even to the extent of the candidate scripting false starts, hesitations and pauses. One candidate went to the length of telling the speaker where to cough! If you find yourself doing this sort of thing — stop. There are ways around the problem, of course. You could 'edit' an interviewee's contribution to the programme, but the phone-in remains a no-go area in all circumstances.

It is not just in the radio-programme transformation that this problem of scripting the unscriptable manifests itself. The 'hot-seating' of a character from a novel or play (sometimes, as part of a radio programme) or placing characters from a novel in the *Big Brother* house, for instance, can lead to the artificiality of writing what would really be impromptu. Even if you are writing a play script or a dramatic monologue as your transformation, you must remember that there is a significant difference between crafted dialogue and the unrehearsed nature of everyday speech. It is usually only linguists who write down (or transcribe) unplanned speech. Your work for Module 5: Talk in Life and Literature will alert you to this fact.

# The commentary

In the commentary you have the opportunity to reflect on what you have achieved in the transformation — your intentions, the processes you went through and the decisions you made. As with the transformation, you must keep a clear focus on your audience, but you will find that this is not as easy to identify. Although your teacher, and possibly a moderator, will read what you have written, it is not always helpful to think of them as the prime audience. Your teacher is likely to know about most of the decisions that informed your transformation, and may have contributed to some of them; the moderator will read your work from a very different perspective — to check whether the marks awarded are appropriate. It may be more helpful to think of other members of your class or of future text transformers as your audience, and try to explain to them as clearly as possible the steps you took to achieve your finished text.

There is no blueprint or formula for commentaries, as the transformations on which they are based are so diverse. What is appropriate to include or to emphasise in one commentary may not be appropriate for another. The source text will be different, the transformed genre will be different and the intentions of each writer will be different, so it would be futile to insist that each commentary follows the same pattern or contains the same observations.

There is much that you could include in your commentary. If you were to write about every aspect of your transformation, then you would comfortably exceed the 2,000 word limit — but you are not expected to do so. The assessment criteria for the commentary state that the most successful commentaries 'focus on the essential, significant aspects of the task' and that 'succinct expression allows a good range of comment, though word limits mean that the candidate cannot comment on everything'.

You have to decide what is *essential* and *significant* in your own transformation. The following sections examine some of the areas that can constitute this good range of comment.

## Aims and intentions

Despite the fact that you will write most, if not all, of your commentary after you have completed your transformation, it is the former that the moderator will read first. The reason for this is quite simple — the moderator wants to understand the aims and intentions of your transformation before he/she reads it. Even if the transformation is enjoyable to read, displays assured control over the appropriate genre conventions and sustains its appeal to the intended audience, the moderator will benefit from reading the commentary first. Otherwise, it is possible that he/she will not find the interplay between the two texts immediately obvious, or may not find your perceptive understanding of the source text directly apparent.

You should use the commentary to clarify your intentions and point out interplay between the two texts, in order to demonstrate that you have produced a thorough and enlightening transformation, and not merely a good piece of original or creative writing. This will enable anyone reading your new text to make an assured judgement about it.

## Source text

You will have good reasons for your choice of source text. You may have enjoyed reading it or you may think that it will provide some profitable opportunities for transformation. Whatever your reasons, it will be assumed that you have a detailed knowledge of the source text, not only of its content but also its discourse (purposes, writer–reader relationships, genre), structure and context. Your commentary should show an understanding of these features where they are relevant to the changes you have made in the transformation.

## Changes

An essential element of text transformation is that you will make changes between the texts, which you must discuss in the commentary. Changes which you might wish to discuss in your commentary include:
- genre
- time
- setting
- context
- character
- perspective and point of view
- register
- structure

- purpose
- reader–writer relationships

Any change you make will be related to your aims and intentions, as noted above. Therefore, the moderator will be looking for clear and effective comments on the purpose and effects of some of the most important ones. Why, for instance, did you change the formal register of *Emma*, the order of events in *Oliver Twist*, the narrative point of view in *Robinson Crusoe*, the genre of 'My Last Duchess', the gullible nature of Othello, the political perspective in *Animal Farm*? It is to these sorts of questions that your commentary should provide quite detailed answers.

## Language

Specific language changes (e.g. grammar, lexis, register) from your source text to your new text are important to mention in your commentary, but they should not be overemphasised to the exclusion of other aspects of your transformation. The commentary is not the place for close linguistic or stylistic analysis of either your source or your new text.

The previous three sections have shown that the main focus of your commentary should be a discussion of the aims, intentions, and discourse of your transformation. In writing about these features, you will automatically have considered some of the language choices and changes you made. It is here, when considering the larger discourse issues of your new text, that you will be writing in some detail about language, but you will be writing *in support* of these other, wider features. If you begin a commentary by immediately analysing language, you risk losing focus on the other, arguably more important, areas. In considering how much emphasis to place on your language choice, remember that one of the descriptors for the top mark band requires candidates to 'demonstrate understanding of the grammatical and lexical choices relevant to the transformation'.

The key word in this descriptor is *relevant*. The parallel descriptor for the next lower mark band is the same, but adds that candidates should not 'over-concentrate on these with a resultant underplaying of the larger discourse issues'.

Candidates in the lowest mark band, however, 'demonstrate little or no awareness of the language choices relevant to the transformation'.

This confirms that you must not either over-emphasise or ignore language completely in your commentary.

# Comments to avoid

There are a number of points of discussion that should be avoided in your commentary, as they gain no marks and give a bad impression overall. Three of these points are considered below.

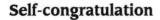

## Self-congratulation

As you draft and redraft your transformation, it is likely that your classmates, friends and family will read your work and offer their comments. However, you must remember that it is your teacher and moderator who will make the final judgement and award a mark. Even if your family and friends loved your work, you must avoid self-congratulatory comments such as 'My mum read it and enjoyed it'. There is nothing to be gained by saying how well you think you have done or how successful you think the final version of your transformation is. Such comments will not influence your teacher or moderator at all.

## If only I had more time!

This is the opposite of self-congratulation. The reader of your commentary is not interested in which source text you wish you had chosen, or the changes and improvements you wanted to make to your final transformation. Your work is judged on the basis of what your teacher or moderator has in front of them, not on what might have been there if you had had that extra week to perfect it. One of the rationales behind coursework is that you *do* have plenty of time in which to produce your best work. Complaining about what you would have done is only going to reflect negatively on your time-management skills.

## Describing what you have done

The heart of any commentary should be the analysis and evaluation of your transformation, together with relevant and succinct supporting evidence for your observations. No one wishes to read an anecdotal account of what you did in the preparation and execution of your work or a summary of its contents. Your teacher and moderator do not require such a summary, as they have your transformation in front of them and will read it themselves.

# Transformations
# and
# Commentaries

This section provides you with two examples of text transformation and their associated commentaries.

The source text of the first transformation is L. P. Hartley's novel *The Go-Between*, and is an article in the style of a leading women's magazine. The article is based on an interview with one of the main characters, Marian Maudsley, as she reflects on the parts of her life detailed in the novel. This submission was awarded an A grade.

The second transformation is a reworking of *A Cream Cracker under the Settee*, one of the monologues in the first series of Alan Bennett's *Talking Heads* television programmes. The candidate has transformed Doris's monologue into a short story and was awarded a D grade for his work overall.

The third transformation is based on T. S. Eliot's poem 'The Journey of the Magi'. In this poem, one of the three wise men (or magi), who travelled to Bethlehem for the birth of Jesus Christ, recalls the events of the journey after a number of years and reflects on the significance of the birth on his life. The choice of travel writing as the new genre is an interesting and potentially successful one. The candidate was awarded a low C grade.

It is important that you do not consider these three examples of submissions as models for your own work. There is a great variety of source texts you can choose for your transformation, a large number of genres to write in, and different approaches to the commentary. The three transformations presented here have been chosen to illustrate the standards of work required to achieve A, C and D grades, but submissions significantly different in approach can also achieve similar grades.

The grades awarded to all three candidates reflect the combined marks for their transformation and the commentary. The transformation and commentary are worth 30 marks each.

Each transformation and commentary is accompanied by moderator comments, preceded by the icon *M*, indicating where credit has been awarded or withheld, and outlining why overall A, C and D grades were awarded. You should pay particular attention to these comments, as they will help you to prepare your own folder of work.

# Transformation and commentary 1

## Transformation from *The Go-Between* to a women's magazine article

# MISS MARIAN MAUDSLEY

The Kobal Collection

Now an old woman, Marian, daughter of the aristocratic Maudsleys, has a lot to recall. In an *exclusive* interview, she gives us an insight into what went on during her young life and how that changed her future. We learn of all the men in Marian's life and finally discover the truth about what exactly *did* go on during that crazy summer of 1900!

As I made my way through the elegant trellises and flowerbeds, I felt as though the summer of 1900 had never left Marian. Her little cottage in the countryside looks weathered and tired, much like Marian herself. Standing in the garden, you could almost forget that you were living in a world of hustle, bustle and technology, although, however beautiful the garden was, I couldn't help but feel a sense of eeriness as I approached the old oak door. Something didn't feel quite right. The windows were laced in dust and glistening cobwebs clung to the chipped wooden window frames.

*M.* The transformation has started well. The writer has included a picture of Marian (from the film of *The Go-Between*), demonstrating that she is aware of th e conventions associated with articles in women's magazines. The introductory paragraph placing the subsequent article in context similarly shows this aware-ness. However, the article does not, as it claims, deal with *all* the men in Marian's life. The candidate would haveexceeded the word limit if she had done so.

As I grasped the brass doorknocker, I took a deep breath. Strange I know, but there was something about the prospect of meeting a lady so different from myself that I found daunting. I'd hardly even knocked once and the door crept open. 'Oh! You're that woman from the magazine, I expect?' Clutching my pen and notepad, I wondered how I could look as though I was from anywhere else!

> *M.* The writer continues to use appropriate genre conventions as she sets the scene for the interview and establishes the uneasiness of the reporter at the prospect of meeting Marian. Details of 'trellises', 'chipped wooden window frames' and the 'brass doorknocker' are effective. However, the perhaps unjustified assumption that readers will recognise Marian, 'daughter of the aristocratic Maudsleys', detracts from the general success of the opening paragraph.

The prospect of the first meeting was something that had been terrifying me for weeks. I expected to be confronted with an elaborate, sherry-drinking 'lady-of-the-manor' type, but now I realised just how stupid I was. Instead Marian looks small and frail. Nothing like her former self. Just like the garden of her countryside home, she is weathered. Beaten by time and brown around the edges. She oozes a sense of lost dreams and regret, a characteristic I picked up before even speaking to her. She leads me into a quaint room. A log fire is burning fiercely and there is a scruffy looking cat sat across the room on a battered armchair. An heirloom from Brandham Hall, perhaps? As interested as I am by my surroundings, I am keen to ask some questions. After accepting her invitation for tea and biscuits, I settle comfortably into the plush sofa by the fire, and I begin…

> *M.* This section is well-written, setting the scene and developing the character of the reporter with a number of suggestive touches, e.g. the way that her expectations are undermined by Marian's 'small and frail' appearance. However, we are by now a considerable way into the article and there has been little engagement with the events of the novel. If the writer continues in this manner, she may fail to provide any enlightening insight into the book.

I am keen to establish what is happening in Marian's life now. As much as she tries to hide it, I can see that Marian is a lonely woman, trapped in a world of times gone by. She tells me that she rarely sees her family and has few friends. Instead she passes the time by reading, sewing and occasionally making the odd sponge cake. Nice, but unfortunately for her she has no one to share it with, except perhaps her pet cat, Winston! For Marian, her future is purely to remember the past and her youth. Although even then, she tells me how she was never really happy. I question why. How could she possibly be unhappy when she had so much: beautiful dresses, a viscount fiancé, a fabulous countryside retreat and a handsome secret lover! Surely that's what we all desire? The perfect life! But it seems Marian's life wasn't so perfect after all!

> *M.* In this paragraph, the writer refers to the novel in more detail, mentioning specific characters. She introduces interplay between the two texts by establishing the poignant contrast between the Marian of the novel and the imagined present-day woman. The moral universe of the source

magazine is revealed in the reporter's unquestioning assumption that what all its readers desire is the same 'perfect life', i.e. one that includes an aristocratic fiancé and a secret lover, together with 'beautiful dresses and a fabulous countryside retreat'. The writer has obviously studied the discourse of the magazine closely and has reproduced it effectively here.

## Family

From a young age, Marian had witnessed a loveless marriage between her parents. They seemed to be together purely due to ease and social expectations rather than love and happiness. Her mother, she tells me, was a cold woman. Never one to tolerate tears and sadness, her policy was simply to brush it under the carpet and forget that problems ever existed.

## 'My father was suppressed by my mother. His life was dictated by her!'

Her father, on the other hand, was a more gentle man, who always tried to solve problems as they arose; he was rarely successful in this quest. Marian tells me he was living almost under 'suppression'. He had no choice but to do as his wife told him!

Unfortunately for Marian, the dictatorial nature of her mother seemed to affect her too. 'I had no choice but to follow my mother's orders,' she tells me. 'At times I wanted to lash out and tell her "No mother!" but it was easier just to keep quiet.' By this point, I am developing a sympathy for Marian that I didn't expect to feel. So often has she been portrayed as a cold old woman, with a distorted view of the world, but I am beginning to feel that maybe it's not all her fault. Her life and behaviour were dictated by her mother, so maybe too were her thoughts and feelings. We'll see…I seem to be developing a better relationship with Marian at this point, so feel it is the right time to ask *the* question. Before she has chance to continue I jump in, 'So, Marian, will you tell me about Ted?'

One of the features of this style of article is that the reporter's personality is often as important as that of the interviewee, and the writer has captured this feature quite well. We become aware of her shifting sympathies and of her developing relationship with Marian. There is clear engagement with the source text — references to Marian and her parents provide an insight into Marian's character and suggests reasons for her affair with Ted Burgess. The writer continues to make close links between the two texts and uses accurate English.

## Ted Burgess

From her pale face and wide eyes I can see that she is shocked, but surely she knew that he was going to come up somewhere. After all, it's what we all want to know, isn't it? 'It all happened a very long time ago' she begins. 'There isn't really very much to say. We courted for some time and then circumstances changed that. Simple!' While Marian sums the story up very simply for me, I know there is more. I ask if she can explain these circumstances for me, and my, oh my, am I in for a shock…On her yearly visits to Brandham Hall, the Maudsley's Norwich retreat, Marian had developed a close relationship with Ted Burgess, the local farmer. This gradually grew to love and, by the summer of 1900, the two lovers couldn't keep their hands off each other.

𝓜 The writer continues to develop Marian's character and provides new perspectives on the source text. We are made more aware of Marian's self-delusion and inability to face the full consequences of her actions. She can offer only an inadequate explanation of what happened — 'circumstances changed that. Simple!'

## 'We couldn't bear to be apart'

'Towards the end, it was a very intense affair,' Marian tells me. 'In truth, we couldn't bear to be apart for more than twelve hours. But sometimes seeing each other just wasn't an option. You must remember, I was engaged to a viscount!' I am keen to find out just where these secret rendezvous took place. Marian tells me that the old outhouses of Brandham Hall were a favourite location. 'It was funny actually, because around the outhouses was *atropa belladonna*. Ted always said I reminded him of them: beautiful but deadly!' Marian giggles. I detect an air of arrogance about her. Looking around at the photos in the room, I can see that Marian was a very beautiful lady. However, not so beautiful is the fact that she's very much aware of this!

𝓜 The writer uses a feature of some women's magazine interviews where the reporter is critical of the subject. This candidate's folder also contained examples of articles from the source magazine — helping the moderator to gauge the authenticity of the voice adopted.

There was still one question puzzling me. Why, when engaged to a viscount, was Marian even remotely interested in the common farmer? She seems to understand what I am saying, but tells me that normality is what she wanted. Throughout her whole life, she had been surrounded by a world of wealth and decadence. Ted was her escape route from that. A person with whom she could totally be herself. There were no mannerisms that the two had to conform to when they were together. They were madly in love and relished the rawness of each other's bodies and personalities.

𝓜 This paragraph gives more insight into the relationship between Marian and Ted. The use of Marian's voice demonstrates the successful change of perspective from that of the novel. *The Go-Between* is in fact narrated by Leo, a boy on the verge of adolescence, who does not really under-stand what is going on or the conse-quences of the tasks Marian asks him to perform. The fact that Marian does not even mention Leo in this interview may reflect her self-absorbedness. The similari-ties between her character in the source and the new text are another strength of this transformation.

## 'With Ted and me, there was no need for the niceties!'

When she was with Ted, Marian wasn't the daughter of the aristocratic Maudsleys, or the fiancée of a viscount; she was simply Marian. From listening to her speak so fondly of Ted, I feel that what resulted from *that* summer was nothing less than a tragedy. It's just so sad that social restrictions and the high expectations of the time meant that these lovers were doomed from the start. However, it's not just the era that was to blame. After all, at times in our own lives I'm sure we can relate to having a lover or partner who, by others' opinions, we shouldn't have been with. However, the consequences for Marian were far greater than any of us could expect.

> *M.* Again, this paragraph reflects the moral perspective of many women's magazines and the interplay between the two texts is engaging. The personality and opinions of the reporter are also clearly on display. However, the penultimate sentence is expressed clumsily. The writer would have benefited from checking her work more carefully.

## Consequences

While enjoying 'each other's company' at their favourite black spot — the outhouses, Ted and Marian faced ultimate humiliation. Marian's mother caught them. Not a woman who would take kindly to what she witnessed. 'It was so humiliating!' exclaims Marian. 'Here's the woman who had raised me from birth, witnessing me in the most compromising of positions. Truly horrendous!' As horrendous as this may have been for Marian, there was still more to come. Shocked at what she saw that day, her mother entered a deep depression, which eventually led to her leaving the family in a desperate attempt to cope. This left Marian shattered. Although her relationship with her mother was not ideal, she was still a woman that Marian needed around. 'Growing up was hard enough,' she tells me, 'but growing up without a mother, well, that was hard. I craved her guidance, support and approval but it simply wasn't there any more!' Marian's words touch me; I feel for her. In

describing this devastating event I can see the sadness in her eyes. It's a deep, lingering hurt that has never really left her since that summer of 1900. She knows as well as I do that the pain will live on until the day she dies. Feeling as though the interview may be coming to an end, I begin to relax. Marian senses this and asks me, 'Well, do you not want to hear what happened to Ted? There is more, you know!'

> *M.* This paragraph introduces new information and perspectives on Marian's situation and character, and makes links between the source and the new text.

## Suicide

This baffled me. I had been briefed up until this point, but didn't expect that there would be any more to say. Little did I know that what I was about to hear was more shocking than I could ever have imagined.

> *M.* By drawing to a conclusion, but saving the best till last, the writer demonstrates control — she has obviously kept in mind the overall structure of the article when planning and drafting. Your submitted folder should contain your drafts so that the moderator can monitor the process of your writing and check for plagiarism.

Foolishly, I imagined that following the humiliation at the outhouses, Ted would merely have gone back to where he came from, his love affair with a beautiful aristocratic girl a mere haze from the past. How wrong I was!

> *M.* The personal voice of the reporter is maintained.

## 'Ted took his own life!'

Following the loss of the girl he loved, Ted too sank into a spiralling depression. It was at his lowest point that, at his bleak farmhouse, he decided to take his own life! It all seems too much for Marian now, who has tears rolling down her wrinkled cheeks. I ask her if she wants to go on. 'Well, we've come this far!' I take that as a yes.

### Learning to cope

From Marian's response, it almost seems like she sees this interview as a therapy session. As if it is a way for her to confront the past. All I hope is that I've done her some good. After all, suppression is never a good thing! As we continue, Marian tells me how Ted just couldn't cope: 'I don't think it was the humiliation, as to be a farmer in that era was a humiliation in itself. No, I think it was me!' This statement surprises me. Was Marian being arrogant, or was she simply saying it as it was, reserving no politeness or modesty? I'll let you decide. I glance across at Marian; she seems tired and weary. It's so easy to forget that she's an incredibly old lady! It is at this point that I decide to try to wrap up the interview. Marian's tears have dried and I wonder if, when I leave her home, she will just slip back into her lonely, depressive state. I really hope not! I hope that what I have delved deep to discover today helps Marian to come to terms with what has happened in her long and remarkable life. As I make my way to the old oak door, she grasps my arm: 'Thank you!' she exclaims, so sincerely. The look on my face tells her she is welcome. If in just two hours, I have managed to change what little time Marian has left on this earth, then I am satisfied my job is done. As I make my way to the car, I turn back. The sun is shining and the birds are singing. And you know what — for the first time in years, I think Marian is too! ✪

*M* The article reaches a well-rounded conclusion, much in the style of the source magazine, although is perhaps a little too sentimental, with both the birds and Marian 'singing'.

*M* **This transformation demonstrates a high level of technical accuracy, though there remains some slightly awkward expression that the candidate should have emended. There is a clear and assured control over the new genre of a women's magazine article, and the writer shows a keen awareness of the interests of the 'new' audience. Occasionally, the demands of writing in this particular genre seem to take precedence over the main purpose of a transformation — to ensure sufficient interplay between the two texts. In the main, however, the new text gives the reader a clear and enlightening perspective on *The Go-Between* and demonstrates some sophisticated interplay.**

**This transformation was awarded a mark of 28 out of 30.**

# Commentary on *The Go-Between* transformation

🖊 The candidate has chosen to write the commentary in sections. This is a sensible
strategy as it is likely to ensure full coverage.

## Choice of text and genre

For my text transformation I decided I wanted to transform a novel, as this would
give me a large amount of content from which to pick and choose, and ultimately
break down to create my transformation. I chose to transform *The Go-Between* by
L. P. Hartley, as it was a text I was familiar with and that I enjoyed. My original idea,
and one that I have stuck with, was that I wanted to transform the novel into a feature
magazine article recalling Marian Maudsley's life and, most importantly, the events
that occurred during the summer of 1900.

🖊 This introductory paragraph is more descriptive than analytical, though the candidate
does provide an explanation of why she chose a novel as her source text.

I felt that choosing a magazine article provided a distinct comparison between genres
and gave me a lot of scope for how I could display my work, using typical magazine
features such as subheadings, pictures and pulling out important pieces of text, e.g.
'My father was suppressed by my mother. His life was dictated by her!' The fact that
*The Go-Between* was a very dated, formal novel, e.g. 'I was no longer satisfied with
the small change of experience which had hitherto satisfied me' (page 76) meant that
I could adopt a far more informal and modern approach. This was a good thing as
the magazines that I was considering using as a style model were all relatively chatty
and modern.

🖊 At the beginning of the paragraph, the candidate highlights the need for the genres of
the source text and the transformation to be distinctly different, although *comparison*
is not quite the right term. The more appropriate term to use would have been *contrast*.
The references to the formal style of *The Go-Between* are unconvincing, as the novel is
not particularly formal. It is far more important to note the generic difference between
the two texts.

My first choice of style model was *OK!* magazine. I felt that this would reflect the
person who Marian was and the aristocratic family from which she came — *OK!* often
features individuals or families who live grand and decadent lives. This suited Marian
perfectly, but when reading through *OK!* I found that Marian's story was not best
placed in such a magazine. While *OK!* reflected Marian's lifestyle, I didn't think that
it was the right magazine to present the topic of affairs and unrequited love. Therefore
I looked to a more 'chatty' magazine that dealt with modern-day issues that are
important and enjoyable to the independent woman of today. It was then that I decided
upon a style model of *Cosmopolitan* magazine, as this was a far better magazine to

place a story dealing with the above mentioned issues. In most issues, *Cosmopolitan* deals with 'taboo' subjects, therefore I felt that such a story would not only be acceptable, but expected by today's modern and powerful women!

> *The candidate cogently explains and justifies her choice of Cosmopolitan as the style model. However, there is no need to comment on the original choice of magazine, as the moderator is not interested in what might have been, but only in the insights into what she has actually written.*

## Selection of material from the original text

From my previous study of *The Go-Between*, I was drawn to the relationship between Leo Colston and Marian. I decided, however, that I wanted to pull something different out of the novel, which is why I decided to focus on Marian, her life and the things that happened to her during the summer of 1900. I felt that this would be more interesting to write about as a lot more people could relate to love and affairs than they could to using a little boy as a 'go-between' in their romantic relationships! However, there were still many branches that I could take: Marian's relationship with her parents; with Trimingham; or with Ted Burgess. It was her affair with Ted that I chose to home in on, as I felt it was a realistic story for the times we live in today. There was a lot of text from the novel that I didn't need, so I used a shortened version to reacquaint myself with the story, and to pick out key areas, e.g. when Ted and Marian are caught in the outhouses, and the reference to Marian being similar to *atropa belladonna*.

> *The candidate shows awareness of the need to restrict the transformation to one aspect of the novel, as there is too much material to use everything. The focus on the illicit relationship between Marian and Ted is a sensible decision, given the nature of the style model. However, you should never work from an abridged version of the text, as this candidate has done. There is always a danger that abridged versions may be inaccurate, and their intended audiences will not be the same as for the full and original texts.*

Dealing with the issue of having an affair gave me a lot of scope for what I could include in my article. I had difficulty deciding whether my article would be sympathetic towards Marian or not. However, my opinions changed naturally throughout the article. In selecting my material, I didn't actually use any quotes from the novel. This was intentional, as I was keen to avoid using anything that may have made my article appear dated, overly formal or otherwise unlike a modern magazine article. Instead I focused on *events* within the novel, such as when Marian and Ted were caught by Mrs Maudsley. Within my mind I had a constant awareness of the novel and the events within it, and I chose to use this more as a base to which I could add depth and substance through the use of Marian's input, shown in the article through the use of quotations, e.g. 'It was so humiliating!'

> *The candidate comments here on the sensible decision not to use any quotations from the novel because they may look out of place in a modern magazine. However, it is untrue to say that the transformation focuses on events alone, as there is a great deal*

about Marian's feelings and character. The last sentence of this paragraph is vague, and 'depth and substance' could have been better defined.

I also found the epilogue particularly helpful while writing my article, as it condensed exactly what had gone on during the infamous summer into manageable sections. It gave me important details, such as the fact that Marian did marry Trimingham and have children etc. I kept this information in mind while producing the article, so that it contained accurate details.

*The candidate's use of the epilogue of The Go-Between shows that she may not have read the full novel recently and possibly relied on summaries to refresh her memory.*

## Linguistic choices

As my piece was a transformation, I was keen to keep away from anything similar to the original piece. This enabled me to adopt a very different writing style from that found in the original novel. In the novel, the text was highly formal, demanding and dated, e.g. 'At last I was free from all my imperfections and limitations; I belonged to another world, the celestial world. I was one with my dream life'. Therefore I decided that in my article I would adopt a far more chatty and informal approach. This gave me the chance to write differently from my normal style, as I had never written in the informal style of a women's magazine. Informality matched my style model perfectly, as the language used in magazines like Cosmopolitan is often easy-going and light-hearted. However, although the language of my model was informal and casual, the approach was still very professional — the writer always managed to get the point across. This was something that I was keen to replicate in my own article. Whilst I wanted my piece to appear unthreatening, I was aware that the topics that I was discussing, e.g. love affairs and suicide, were not light-hearted and therefore required an amount of professionalism and seriousness in their discussion. I feel that I have achieved this in my article, e.g. 'Following the loss of the girl he loved, Ted too sunk into a spiralling depression. It was at his lowest point...he decided to take his own life...Marian...has tears rolling down her wrinkled cheeks.'

*You should use the commentary to write about the reasons for some of your language choices. This candidate has already mentioned contrasts of formality in a previous paragraph, so it would have been better to restrict language comments to this section in order to avoid repetition. The candidate should also have provided some particular examples of the informal style used in the article and analysed exactly how this informality was achieved. When she does quote from her work (at the end of the paragraph), she lets the quotations stand alone, without examining how her language choices help achieve the desired professional style.*

I am happy that I have achieved an adequate balance of informality and seriousness. The quote above shows how I dealt sympathetically and respectfully with awkward discussion points, whereas the text below highlights the differences in my linguistic choices, and shows how I can change my language use and tone to suit the varying degrees of seriousness in individual situations, e.g. 'I expected to be confronted with an elaborate, sherry-drinking, 'lady-of-the-manor' type.' This quote is rather light-hearted and is an example of how I managed to keep my language simple yet effective — such a sentence provokes many thoughts and images in my mind as to what an elaborate sherry-drinker is like! The use of rhetorical questions was part of my linguistic choice. I asked them so that I could engage the reader and make them feel involved in what was going on, e.g. 'I'm sure we can relate to having a lover...who...we shouldn't have been with.'

*This paragraph focuses on the two differing writing styles in the article. It is a sensible and appropriate focus and is supported by quotations, e.g. the observation about the use of rhetorical questions. The paragraph would, however, have benefited from closer analysis of the quotations.*

A final linguistic feature was to create a sense of modern day 'cool'. I wanted my article to appear as though the write-up had just rolled off my tongue, almost as though I was recalling the story whilst speaking to a friend, for example. This modern-day 'cool' is so prevalent in today's magazines and, although perhaps slightly pretentious, it was the style I wanted to adopt as I felt as though it would make my article more realistic and effective, and ultimately mimic the articles in my style model.

*The candidate successfully characterises the intended style of the article. However, it would have been useful to provide examples of this style, together with some analysis of how it had been achieved. The ability of the candidate to write sensibly and at some length about her linguistic choices, while using generally appropriate terminology, is a positive feature of this commentary. She writes at an appropriate length on this aspect of her work and has not allowed the commentary to become solely a linguistic analysis. Her comments in this section are an attempt to illuminate the choice she made. Overall, the commentary is well balanced.*

## Structure and organisation of the transformation

My style model was *Cosmopolitan*, and therefore I wanted the structure of my article to imitate the structure of articles in this magazine. I found a recent interview with Natalie Imbruglia (see Appendix), and used this as a template for structuring my own work. I decided to include a large photograph of Marian in her younger days on my first page. To this I added just a short introduction and that was my opening page complete. This was simple yet effective as the boldness and brightness of the full-sized photograph would probably be enough to attract the attention of potential readers, and the brief and manageable introduction provides a short insight to the article, enabling potential readers to make an informed decision as to whether they want to read on.

*It is always important to spend some time in the commentary on the overall structure and organisation of the transformation. The candidate does so in this paragraph, referring to her style model in order to illustrate some of the genre conventions she has tried to incorporate into the article. The candidate's inclusion of an actual*

*Cosmopolitan* article in her submitted folder is helpful. It allows the moderator to assess the validity of the commentary's claims about style and structure.

I then divided the rest of the work into two columns with relatively small text; I felt this looked more professional and accurately replicated my style model. From time to time I used features such as subheadings to inform the reader what was going to be discussed in the following paragraphs. The use of subheadings was a feature I had noticed in *Cosmopolitan*. I also pulled out important pieces of information that Marian was telling the reporter, so that they were bold and eye-catching, e.g. 'Ted took his own life!' This is again a structural feature of *Cosmopolitan*.

*M.* Discussions of layout and presentation will never be awarded many marks. Candidates who over-concentrate on these aspects will find it difficult to achieve the higher marks.

When it came to producing my article, I simply used the beginning, middle and end format. I opened the piece with a long and descriptive introduction and then used the original novel as a base for the progression of my discussion with Marian. That is, I didn't just jump straight into her affair with Ted; instead I established her as an individual that my readership could identify with. Despite the fact that she was probably approximately forty years older than the readership of *Cosmopolitan*, she still had her own ideas and values, which were similar to those of modern women.

*M.* The candidate has made an obvious mistake here — Marian would be about 123 years old in 2005.

I then progressed to her life now, in 2005, and after discussing this and forming the foundations of Marian's personality and character, I felt it was a suitable time to revert to the past. I started with her family relationships. To be truthful, I left the best until last, when Marian and Ted were caught having sex, followed by Ted's suicide. Leaving the main event until last is a feature that I have noticed many magazines adopt, including *Cosmopolitan*, so I decided that I would do the same in an attempt to make my article as realistic as possible. After dropping the 'bombshell' I began to tie up the article, drawing my own conclusions and identifying my own thoughts and feelings. This is something that I hoped my readership would do too. The end of the article is a perfect time to make decisions about what they think of Marian and her story etc. I had developed more and more sympathy as the article went on, so I wrote slightly biased towards Marian in my closing sentences. However, I didn't do this in an attempt to sway the reader; instead I wanted to show my individuality and personal choice. I hope that through my article, my readership were able to evaluate what they had read, and so to do the same.

*M.* The commentary is brought to a close with a detailed justification of the ending of the article. These final comments form an effective conclusion to the commentary.

*M.* **This is a full commentary, focusing on most of the significant aspects of the transformation. The candidate's comments are clear and usually effective, demonstrating intelligent reflection and analysis. The scrutiny of the overall structure of** the article is particularly strong, as is the replication of the codes and conventions of women's magazine articles. The commentary could have been improved by more detailed attention to and examination of the language choices made in the article.

The commentary, however, is not as strong as the transformation and was awarded 26 marks.

# Transformation and commentary 2

## Transformation from a *Talking Heads* monologue to a short story

### *A Cream Cracker under the Settee*

Bang, bang, bang. This was the noise Doris had put up with all morning, the same repeated noise over and over, and she knew it would carry on all the afternoon.

*The language of this paragraph is very close to that of the source text. A moderator would question how much actual transformation has taken place.*

Nobody ever came and nobody ever went, oh except Zulema, but if Doris had her way, she wouldn't either.

The noise of the banging gate had become more of a rhythm. Doris sat impatiently. It seemed that patience was a virtue that Doris had been at the back of the queue for, and if anyone had found this out it was poor old Wilfred, by the sound of Doris you wouldn't think for a second that she was an extremely frail old lady of 75 with an even frailer pacemaker, who was often prone to the odd bout of dizzy spells.

*The final sentence of this paragraph is long and clumsy. It is difficult to follow and suggests that the writer has not checked his work carefully.*

Doris, an extremely stubborn lady, who could argue the hind legs off a donkey, would rather have you believe she was just a mature 21-year-old trapped in the body of someone aged 84.

*Doris is not 84. Alan Bennett makes it clear that she is in her seventies, and the candidate has already referred to her as 75 in the preceding paragraph. This suggests a lack of care.*

She picked up the large glass-framed picture fondly and cradled it as if it were a newborn baby. As she took in every ounce of memory that the battered old frame held, she heard the echoing of the wedding bells that had filled her with such an immense joy that day.

Strange how on looking back we have such blinkered visions. In reality the 'frail' old Doris had near enough nagged poor old Wilfred into his grave. As she snapped back to reality, she noticed the thick blanket of dust that enveloped the edges of the aging frame, as she placed it tenderly back on the hook.

*In this paragraph, the candidate tells us outright about Doris's nagging. This is not as effective as Alan Bennett's technique, where Doris reveals things about herself without realising that she is doing so. The candidate clearly does not consider what made Alan Bennett's original monologue so effective and therefore produces a weak transformation. You should always consider the strengths of a source text before embarking on your transformation.*

Doris was an extremely proud woman who hated the thought of dust and dirt anywhere, but the milk she had put on to boil was producing a large billowing cloud of steam from within the kitchen, giving every indication that it was about to evaporate. So she hurried along to the very small yet immaculate kitchen, forgetting for now about the frame.

*Doris is unable to hurry anywhere. The candidate should have remembered that in the source text she has broken her hip and is lying on the floor, unable to move without great difficulty.*

By the time Doris had eventually made her way into the kitchen, the medium-sized black pan looked more like an intricate water feature from an ornate garden. The white bubbling milk splashed and spluttered over the sides of the pan. It settled on the prehistoric contraption that vaguely resembled a cooker of some description.

Wilfred had always said he would get around to fitting a brand new cooker. He had seen Doris gazing longingly at the sparkling new kitchens in a copy of 'modern' home magazine one Tuesday, and had decided to put it on his 'to do' list.

Doris had often wondered exactly what this 'list' to which he so often referred was. She had never seen such a list. That would count as organisation and organisational skills were something that Wilfred was distinctly lacking in. She gazed at the burnt brown stains on the cooker. Gazing and daydreaming were two things that she did most of the time. After all she had little else to occupy her mind. No husband, no children. 'Children' was a subject that had been brushed under the carpet and disregarded in Doris and Wilfred's house, all those years ago. Painful, painful memories then. Memories that still pained her even now.

*The candidate has successfully picked up on a number of themes and ideas from the source text, e.g. Wilfred's 'to-do list' and Doris's miscarriage referred to later in the text.*

Still gazing at the cooker, Doris wondered why she had put the milk on to boil, she couldn't for the life of her remember why and now she just wished that she hadn't bothered.

The encrusted mess made Doris's skin crawl. 'Let it wait' Zulema would have said, 'it won't kill you'.

Doris's eyes flicked and danced in excitement as she looked about the kitchen like a nervous child. Zulema wasn't here now and she'd never know, what harm could it do? So Doris opened the ivory-glossed cupboard, and pulled out a pad of shiny wire wool.

The scratching sound of metal on metal rang through the kitchen, and the brown stain on the cooker was no more.

Doris awoke with a shudder; she uncurled from her large armchair. It was dark outside, but she had no idea of the time or of how long she had been asleep. There was a chill in the air, almost a ghostly chill but then she looked up at the large bay window, with its un-drawn curtains that were billowing in the cold winter wind.

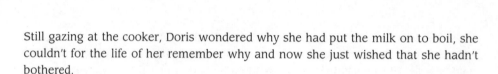 We had not been given any indication that Doris had fallen asleep. It is always important to check your work thoroughly to ensure that no contradictions remain (such as the earlier mistake about Doris's age) or that vital information about plot or events has been overlooked, as here.

She could stand it no longer; she got up onto the buffet and clambered up. As she shut the window she could see the leaves coming down outside, she would not of cared if they were her leaves but they weren't, they were next door's leaves coming right down onto her path!

This paragraph shows the need for careful proofreading. The candidate should have written 'would not have', not 'would not of'.

Doris hated this, in her mind anyone walking by would see the path and form judgements about her. They would think she was incapable, senile even! That would really please social services and she would be tucked away once and for all in Stafford House. She snatched the curtains shut in a fit of proud defiance.

And then it started, would she ever get a peaceful break, bang, bang, bang she thought it had blown shut but there it was as always, bang, bang, bang. The sneck was loose, yet another thing Doris was prohibited from trying to fix. The welfare would have a field day, and once again the thought of life locked away in Stafford House niggled at the back of Doris's mind.

However much she resented home help, or 'home hindrance' as she called it, it was the only thing standing between her and the indignity of existence in a residential home, and Zulema was bearable, just.

Zulema would have just ordered Doris 'to pull her horns in and swallow a little pride else risk losing it all'.

Doris was feeling a little put out and agitated by the noise of the gate, so she went to bed. When she awoke Zulema had already let herself in and was busying herself dusting the furniture. Doris disliked it when Zulema dusted. Dusted? You couldn't call it that. Zulema does not dust, she only half dusts, she flicks at the furniture!

*In the original text, Zulema remains an off-stage figure, described only through Doris's words. To make a more effective transformation, the candidate could have written from Zulema's point of view — this would have given us a different perspective on Doris herself.*

Barney sprinted along Doris's garden leaving a trail of charming little presents, a series of rather large holes, and one rather large bone, which appeared to be the remains of one rather large pork chop!

Barney was the next-door neighbour's large golden retriever, playful, energetic and full of curiosity. 'Curiosity killed the cat' Doris thought to herself, and Barney's garden antics only served to confirm that Doris had been right not to let Wilfred have a dog.

*The candidate expands upon the relationship between Doris and her husband.*

Wilfred had always been hankering after a dog, she had not been keen. Hairs and all up and down, then having to take it out every minute, she would have been the one taking the flea-bitten animal out for walks, feeding and playing with it.

However, the news of an impending addition to the family had been a distraction, and he had begun fiddling with lumps of wood and metal in a vague attempt to make forts and various other toys.

*Again, the candidate uses details from the original text effectively (Wilfred's desire to make toys for his unborn child).*

A tear welled up in her eye, but Doris being Doris she quickly dismissed it.

Do not get me wrong, Doris would have you believe that she was a heartless, uncaring and unemotional.

*'Do not get me wrong' is the first indication of the narrator's voice. Until this point, the third-person narrator has remained in the background — this direct address to the reader is intrusive and unsuccessful, especially as it is the only time in the transformation that the voice is used. This suggests that the writer is not fully in control of the piece, and that it should have been edited more stringently.*

If you met her, at first glance you would barely see her for the large chip that she carried on her shoulder. However Doris's looks were extremely deceiving. Once you broke through the harsh outer exterior, you could see that she was just a very old lady, who refused to let loneliness in. If she didn't let her guard down, age wouldn't catch her out.

She found herself in the hallway. This is where the pram had stood. Doris had always moaned about the fact that it blocked the door. Wilfred and Doris had been so proud, maybe a little eager. It had been a real pram, springs, a hood, and large shiny silver wheels. Wilfred had spotted it in the *Evening Post*; he had gushed with a beaming ray of paternal pride.

'Don't let's jump the gun,' Doris had said, ever the voice of compromising reason. Wilfred had won her over, it had been an irresistible pram and Doris couldn't resist having the best. It would have been the chance of a lifetime. Their chance, their baby, their happiness.

She once again glanced over at the place where the pram had stood. She had wanted to see him, cuddle him and kiss him, but when she had awoke, the stifling pain in her stomach choked her, she had wanted to call out, but he had gone. Taken from her all too soon, without having known his mother, she would have made a marvellous mother, they would have made marvellous parents, maybe even grand-parents.

They'd wrapped him in newspaper. Newspaper?

Chips were wrapped in newspaper not babies. They'd said he wasn't a baby, but he was, to Doris he was.

'We are better off love,' Wilfred had said. After that it was never the same between Doris and her beloved Wilfred.

Something niggled at the back of Doris's mind. The very same irritating feeling that had plagued Doris for a few days now, ever since she had spilt the milk. Then it came to her, the picture!

She lifted the picture once again off its hook. Zulema had said she had dusted, but Doris knew that she would not have done it properly, she never did. The thick blanket of dust that she had noticed only days earlier still coated the edges of the frame. Doris hated dust.

Once again climbing onto the buffet, she set about the dusting, only this time her grip faltered and the precious frame fell to the floor shattering into thousands of crystal-like fragments taking poor old Doris with it!

Silence. She lay there, still as a corpse, for several minutes. She could see something under the settee, something out of place. A cream cracker! A cream cracker under the settee. Zulema! She had always been a lazy waste of space.

Her mind drifted and went blank. When Zulema came three days later, Doris still lay there. Peaceful, but no longer alone, reunited with poor Wilfred and their baby. Content. Satisfied. Loved. Something that Doris had not been for along time.

🕮 This is an overly sentimental ending, out of character with Alan Bennett's original text.

🕮 In his introduction to *Talking Heads* Alan Bennett writes about the television monologue form that:

*...there is a single point of view, that of the speaker alone with the camera, and with the rest of the story pictured and peopled by the viewer more effort is demanded of the imagination. In this sense to watch a monologue on the screen is closer to reading a short story than a play. Admittedly it is a stripped down version of a short story.*

With this comment, Alan Bennett neatly indicates the weakness of this transformation — there is not really enough transformation going on. We learn little, if anything, new about Doris's life or character and there can be only a pedestrian amount of interplay between the two texts. The story is competent, if a little dull and unsubtle, although there are some occasionally successful touches. If the candidate had written the story from an entirely different point of view, such as that of Zulema or even of Wilfred, he would have given himself the chance of gaining a higher mark. More careful proofreading would also have been advisable.

This transformation was awarded 13 marks.

■ ■ ■

# Commentary on *Talking Heads* transformation

*A Cream Cracker under the Settee* is one of six monologues written by Alan Bennett for the BBC in 1987.

The monologues were fundamentally devised for an adult viewing/listening television audience and consist of light-hearted, comic views based upon Alan Bennett's observations of the typically British way of life. The Bennett monologues all appear to empathise with and reflect the point of view of the underdog, presented with touching reality.

The primary purpose of Bennett's work is to entertain, but there is also a sense that he is trying to inform about the morals and ethics of society.

*✍ The candidate fails to prove this assertion.*

After reading the Alan Bennett monologues I chose to transform my favourite, *A Cream Cracker under the Settee.* This is the one I enjoyed the most, and I felt that any reader of this monologue would be able to relate to or empathise with the main character Doris, as almost anyone would know someone that reminded them of her. To enable me to transform the text I had to gain a deeper understanding of the plot and its underlying issues.

*M* This claim is not borne out by what has been written in the transformation. As already noted, the main weakness of the transformation is that there is insufficient difference between the two texts.

The monologue is written from the sole viewpoint of an elderly lady named Doris.

*M* Monologues are by definition written from a single, usually self-deluding, viewpoint.

As a character she comes across to the audience as being extremely stuck in her ways, proud, stubbornly defiant, cold and obsessively compulsive. As the monologue develops, Bennett almost allows the audience to catch a glimpse of the real Doris and I felt that this was something I wanted to capture within my transformation.

Doris appears to have been through much emotional turmoil: she and her husband Wilfred lost a baby, which had a detrimental effect on their relationship; her husband then passed away leaving Doris alone and in the hands of the welfare and social services who are often presented as the demons of society. This serves to form much of Doris's edgy personality. Therefore I aimed to retain as much of this as possible in the transformation.

*M* The candidate comes close here to acknowledging that little transformation has taken place.

The key themes running through the text would at first appear very simple but after analysis it becomes apparent that they are in fact very perplexing. The themes appear to mirror Bennett's own personal attitudes towards society, as most of his works feature the recurring themes of abuse, neglect, social issue, and the ethics of the social services. Due to the complexity of these themes they form the basis of the majority of the subtext. Marital relationships, miscarriage, old age, loneliness, and obsession are the main themes, attitudes and values that Bennett incorporates into *A Cream Cracker under the Settee*.

*M* The candidate appears to be writing a 'literary' essay on Alan Bennett's themes and ideas, instead of addressing the issues of the transformation itself. This is not what a commentary should be.

Doris feels let down by Wilfred's reaction to her miscarriage as he seems to shrug it off. This leads to the hardening of Doris's character and is something that I tried to emulate in the transformation. Through her obsessive compulsion with cleanliness and how people view her it would appear that under the surface Doris is fairly insecure, she holds the view that everyone is out to trick her into giving up her freedom and move into a residential home — 'Wouldn't she be better off in Stafford House?'

Although the lexis in the original is moderately simple, it is straight to the point and reflects the extremely direct opinion of the author conveyed through the main character, Doris.

The syntax structure is very short and again direct. This gives the speech a rather punchy, brusque edge. Another effect of this is that the speech appears rushed, which is ironic as Doris has very little, if any, reason to rush her speech. The tone of the language used by Doris therefore is rather blunt, which serves to confirm the nature of her character, for example: 'Hey. Get out. You little demon.'

🖉 We are now halfway through the commentary and there has been little insight shown into the transformation or the processes leading to its creation.

I felt that this monologue lent itself extremely well to transformation. My first thought was that it could be transformed into a play script, but as the original monologue had already been written for television, I did not feel as though it would give me as much creative licence as transforming it into a short story.

🖉 Writing about what other options were considered for the transformation will earn no marks. The moderator is interested in the 'how' and 'why' of what has actually been written.

For a contemporary readership, I felt that a short story would be more suitable, and would allow the use of a more descriptive lexis.

🖉 The candidate should have backed up this assertion.

Transforming *A Cream Cracker under the Settee* into a short story allowed me to maintain the original use of the subtext that almost characterises the comic style of Alan Bennett. I felt that this could be achieved by using an omniscient narrative voice — not only to convey the innermost thoughts, feelings and inhibitions of the character Doris, but also to manipulate a sense of suspense within the audience. This allows the reader to develop their own attitudes and opinions on the events unfolding before them.

🖉 These are empty comments — the content of the transformation does not justify these claims. You must focus your commentary on what you have actually written in the transformation.

In the transformation itself the character Doris was kept very much the same, the aim was to capture the characteristics displayed in the original.

🖉 The candidate has not realised that this is a major flaw of the transformation — that there are very few changes.

One of the main changes that I made was to the lexis used in the story. In contrast to the original, my lexis choices were more descriptive.

🖉 On the contrary, there is little 'descriptive lexis' in the candidate's story apart from the one that he is about to refer to.

I wanted the audience to feel as if they were actually present in the house in which the story unfolds. I used similes to achieve this, e.g. 'by the time Doris had eventually made her way into the kitchen, the medium-sized pan looked more like an intricate water feature'. The repetition of Doris's actual name throughout the transformation served to allow the audience to identify with the fact that it was her story.

The tripartites incorporated into the language allow the semantics of the words to be of more importance to the intended audience, also creating a rhythm within the writing, 'content, satisfied, loved' or 'their chance, their baby, their happiness'.

*The meaning of this sentence is unclear. Avoid making grand observations with no substance — they will not gain you any marks.*

Repetition of lexis is another feature employed in the transformation, again adding importance and definition to what is presented to the reader. The syntax structure of the original, as mentioned previously, was short and reasonably direct. In my transformation of *A Cream Cracker under the Settee* I aimed to include a mixture of long descriptive sentences and short to the point ones. I felt this would have a greater impact and effect on the audience, whilst also breaking up large quantities of descriptive lexis. I maintained the use of subtext within the transformation as I felt that this was one of the characteristics that almost stylised the original. This allowed me to imply events that were about to unfold. For example, in the case of Doris's miscarriage, the use of ongoing subtext allowed me to imply from the beginning that Doris wanted a child, e.g 'cradled it as if it were a new born baby'. This is again reinforced in a future passage where it is apparent that Doris lives alone as Wilfred has died and there were no children. The storyline is finally exposed when it is subsequently implied that she has suffered a miscarriage: 'They wrapped him in newspaper. Newspaper? Chips were wrapped in newspaper not babies.' The main themes were taken directly from the original but were modified slightly to fit with the genre of a short story narrative. The use of subtext in some places also allows for a sarcastic tone, as I wanted the reader to be able to imagine that the words were coming directly from Doris herself. As the original text was a monologue, the audience would have felt as if the main character was speaking directly to them. It was my aim to retain this feature, as I wanted the audience to be able to identify with Doris.

*The candidate is unaware that this aim undermines the purpose of transformation.*

I intended to manipulate the audience's opinion of Doris closely, at first wanting them to respond to Doris with little or no empathy, only to shift their opinion of her completely towards the end as it becomes clear that she is just a lonely old lady.

*It is clear from the start that Doris is a lonely old lady. The audience's opinion may deepen but it wouldn't shift.*

On the whole, I feel I achieved this. Looking back, if I could make any changes to the transformation, I think I would develop the other characters more and make them more defined. I think the characters of Wilfred and Zulema could have been more effectively developed, e.g. by voicing Wilfred's feelings towards the miscarriage.

📖 Here the candidate may be beginning to realise that all was not well with the transformation and that the decision to write a short story based on Doris's viewpoint was flawed. His suggestions as to what he might have done would have been likely to result in a more successful piece of work.

On the whole, I think that *A Cream Cracker under the Settee* converted to short story form is very effective, as the monologue structure of the original lent itself extremely well to transformation. It also allowed the further development of ideas presented in the original.

📖 These concluding comments are rather vague and self-congratulatory.

📖 **Although this commentary is quite lengthy, it is not very successful. The candidate concentrates far too much on the source text, giving little attention to the actual transformation. Because the short-story genre is similar to the television monologue genre, it is only possible to make limited comment on the discourse. Language is not discussed in significant depth, and when it is, it is descriptive rather than analytical. However, the candidate does discuss the aims and intentions of the transformation, and shows sympathetic insight into Doris's character.**

**This commentary falls into the mark band described as demonstrating 'some competent work' (11–15 marks) and was awarded 12 marks.**

# Transformation and commentary 3
## Transformation from 'The Journey of the Magi' to a travelogue

📖 The candidate's choice of source text is an acceptable one as this is a challenging and substantial poem. Using Bill Bryson's style as a model for the transformation into a piece of travel journalism is a good idea.

### Notes from the Middle East

I've known it to be said that it is better to travel than it is to arrive,

📖 The inclusion of this type of clichéd writing is appropriate to the new genre.

but in the case of my latest journey, both travelling and arriving were as bad as each other. My journeys this month took me to the Middle East.

On first impressions then, what a terribly awful place. I'll start with the travelling and the great amount of it we had to do. Now first, I was under the impression that Israel was a hot country. Well, it wasn't.

> The candidate's use of the conversational, colloquial voice here (and throughout the piece) is a successful attempt to mirror the style model. It certainly makes for the 'easy reading' that characterises much travel writing.

Now maybe that's just my bad luck because it was cold. No, it was damned cold and it snowed, a lot. It reminded me of a quotation I know of, from Lancelot Andrewes in 1622: 'A cold coming we had of it, just the worst time of year for a journey, and such a long journey. The ways deep and the weather sharp. The very dead of winter.'

> The inclusion of this quotation from Bishop Lancelot Andrewes (an important seventeenth-century scholar and priest) is introduced awkwardly. T. S. Eliot uses the quotation in his poem, but here it seems out of character with the personality of the 'writer' of the travelogue. It seems unlikely that such a writer would have been familiar with the quotation. The candidate would have done better to allude more informally to the cold weather the 'writer' was experiencing.

As if the weather wasn't enough of a disappointment, we travelled by camels. This just speaks for itself, doesn't it? Camels aren't exactly the friendliest of animals. They spit. A lot. And also, it struck me that their species has yet to evolve properly enough to walk correctly. Because they don't, you know, walk properly. They constantly rock from side to side and make you feel that you are suffering from a bad case of seasickness.

> This section is more in keeping with the jocular and conversational approach of much travel writing, including Bill Bryson's, and is therefore more successful than the use of the Lancelot Andrewes quotation above.

I mentioned to the Magi that maybe a nice jeep or something would have been the better option, but they looked at me with great disdain and the camel men continued to moan...

> The Magi have not been introduced until this point and some explanation as to what they are would have been helpful.

In fact, the camel men moaned so much that eventually they went on strike. Which brought a complete halt to our tedious journey that I had been praying would come to an end as quickly as possible (and I'm not even slightly religious).

> The candidate is at pains to construct a character (or persona) for the travel writer that is modern and unlike that of the Magi. This character is frequently self-deprecating and the candidate uses this to create a humorous contrast between the events of Eliot's poem and the more contemporary, secular approach taken in the transform-ation. Here the device is fairly successful, but there are other occasions when it becomes intrusive and grating.

We ended up in a small, poverty-stricken town. The towns we stopped in were often hostile and there was a great lack of shelter.

*Here the candidate is using Eliot's own words and has much more successfully incorporated them into the new text. There is no sense that the narrative has to stop in order to include them.*

The Magi assured me that all was normal. 'Well, what is the definition of normal? I replied. Trying to be philosophical for a moment and regretting it when they gave me another distasteful stare.

*Again, this shows the contrast between the character of the 'writer' and those of the Magi.*

Anyway, the camel men were still moaning, although, in my opinion, they seemed to be having a very good time of it, unlike me that is. They spent ninety percent of their time drinking and calling for women. Vulgar men they were and travelling with such people brought a negative outlook to the countries we passed through, shame really. These women they called for were silken girls who kept on bringing us all this sherbet. The Magi seemed to enjoy the girls' company a bit too much and surely the Magi should know better than to fraternise with such people (isn't it against their religion?). The prices in these towns were very high considering they were such impoverished communities.

*This section contains some good reworking of the details of Eliot's original (the silken girls and the camel drivers, for example).*

I couldn't quite believe how much basic necessity were costing me, such as eating and shelter, and being that I'm not a lottery winner; I found these prices quite shocking.

*Throughout the transformation, there is evidence of a lack of careful proofreading. In this sentence, for example, the candidate has written 'basic necessity' instead of 'basic necessities'. The use of a semicolon after 'lottery winner' is also incorrect — the candidate should have used a comma. Minor errors such as these, which could have been corrected easily with careful proofreading, detract from the effectiveness of the finished piece.*

The nights were hard because there was not sufficient shelter for us all and it seemed that the Magi were incapable of keeping a fire going and so it was freezing, as I had become accustomed to. However, once the camel men had decided to end their strike, we set off again on our tedious journey and the Magi, in all their wisdom, decided that we should travel at night and sleep in snatches. So now, not only was I on a journey that did not seem to have any real purpose or meaning, I was now being denied my sleep. At this point of the journey, all I could think was how foolish and poorly organised it was and I wish I'd never come.

We arrived in a serene, temperate valley a week later at dawn. This valley seemed slightly warmer and was picturesque with its water mill and running stream. I would recommend this part of the country to anyone who was thinking of visiting the Middle East.

*The candidate is following the structure of the source text closely — events occur in the same order in both texts. The recommendation to visit 'this part of the country' is typical of the genre of travel writing.*

At this point I nearly decided the journey had bee

*This is a further example of the lack of careful proofreading in this piece. Moderators expect a high standard of accuracy in candidates' folders, as there is plenty of time in a coursework module to ensure that submissions are entirely free from errors or typos. The slips of the pen that usually go unpenalised in a timed examination are not treated so leniently in coursework.*

worth it as I sat on my camel and watched a white horse gallop in the distance. But the Magi disturbed the tranquillity when they began acting rather oddly at the sight of three trees (had they never been exposed to wildlife before or were they just nature enthusiasts?). We made our way to a tavern that seemed to me to be more of a gambling house, which the Magi were simply ecstatic about and began to gamble. These are the men who are supposed to be wise and religious and I worried for their sanity. They bet all of that fancy jewellery they wore and lost it, and after all that, it had been a waste of time because nobody had any information at the tavern anyway.

We arrived that evening. Where? You may wonder, well that I could not say. We witnessed the birth of a tiny babe and then it was over. I could very well see a child born in my own country if I wished, but something told me to silence my clever remarks. 'Birth or death?', the Magi asked each other. None knew the answer. Could it be that this journey had some sort of other purpose? I did not know. It certainly had not been a holiday. I didn't even have a tan, so what then? As the Magi set back for their own kingdoms, they muttered something about a loss of identity. Surely they did not mean they had lost their passports?

*This is an example of the less successful use of the jocular, secular narrator. Someone who claimed to be familiar with the works of Lancelot Andrewes would not be puzzled by 'loss of identity', as the narrator claims to be here. The humour has become flat-footed by this point.*

To conclude, in my opinion to visit the Middle East is to be left with questions not answered. Do not visit if you require a relaxing holiday and a tan. Only for that tranquil valley would I return.

## Return to the Middle East

Sam Weston returns to the Middle East in the new millennium and asks 'has anything actually changed?'

🖉 The source poem concludes with a paragraph reflecting on the significance of the journey and the birth of Jesus Christ. Presumably, the candidate has included this section in which the travel writer returns to the Middle East, in order for her to reflect on what she has seen. In the poem, the Magi return to their kingdoms, which they cannot view in the same light as before their visit to Bethlehem. On their journey, they pass through the same towns, not deliberately setting out to revisit them as Sam Weston does. The transformation simplifies the effect of the original, with this final section having a 'tacked-on' feel.

Call me mad but I just couldn't help wondering how, or if, the Middle East had changed since my visit there 3 years ago. Naturally I wasn't looking forward to it after my rather disastrous journey last time, but curiosity got the better of me. I arrived in the kingdom of the Magus, the one who had been so confused over birth and death the last time I was there, on the Friday afternoon. 'Set down this', was what he said on my arrival. Set down what exactly? The lovely warm cup of coffee that I was clutching? Surely not, or did he mean my suitcase, jolly polite if he did.

🖉 The humour has become forced here.

He carried on regardless of the fact I had no idea of what he was talking about. 'Birth or death?' Well yes, I'd heard all this before but what had changed? It seemed that nothing had.

We revisited the hostile cities and, yes, they were still hostile.

🖉 Again, this is not what Eliot is saying in the source poem. He is reflecting on how the birth of Jesus has made the Magi feel uneasy with their old way of life. There is a sense that the candidate has not quite understood the poem or has not been able to incorporate these serious aspects into the chosen genre of a light-hearted travelogue.

You would assume, wouldn't you, that things may have become more commercialised in the length of time I'd been gone but, no, even the sherbet had run out. The silken dresses those women wore were now tatty, I assume they had no money to buy new ones and much to my horror, the camel men were still hanging about and still moaning.

'Alien kingdoms', the Magus came out with. What exactly was he talking about? Alien kingdoms?

'Star Trek?' I guessed.

🖉 Again, the humour is forced here.

He was definitely trying to tell me something but the locals were trying to sell me some tat and at their prices I wasn't going to buy a thing.

'It was all a long time ago', he continued.

'What? The aliens?' I checked. He was clearly upset but how could I help when he was speaking of the supernatural?

'I'm afraid it's not my speciality, maybe you should watch *The X-Files*?' Then it struck me. Do they have televisions in the Middle East? I'd be jolly surprised if they did. I scurried into the nearest tavern to make enquiries. I couldn't see a television anywhere but the highly illegal gambling was still going on which I thought might cheer up the Magus. I called him in and as he trundled up to the bar, he muttered, 'I should be glad of another death'. If he meant me, then that was just out of order. If he disliked me that much he could just bloody well send me home.

As it turned out, it wasn't long before I left anyway. It seemed like I was having one long déjà vu, because everything was scarily the same. I didn't even bother going to that temperate valley I had enjoyed so much before. What was the point? I'd seen it all before. Poor old Magus though, something was definitely troubling him.

*This slightly flat ending to the transformation is probably caused by the difficulty of having a secular and flippant persona deal with highly significant religious issues. There is a mismatch between the two.*

**Overall, this is a very competent transformation. There are few problems of expression, but more careful proofreading would have eliminated the few technical inaccuracies. The choice of genre had potential, but as the transformation progressed, the lack of subtlety became apparent. The candidate showed some understanding of Eliot's original poem, but the theological and religious insights demonstrated in the poem were not explored in the transformation. To have done so would have been challenging, given the genre of the new text and the persona of the writer. There was, however, some successful interplay between the two texts. This transformation was awarded 19 marks.**

■ ■ ■

# Commentary on 'The Journey of the Magi' transformation

The text that I have transformed for this module is a poem by T. S. Eliot, 'The Journey of the Magi'. The poem tells the story of the three wise men to the birth of Jesus in Bethlehem. Throughout the poem, there is a clear sense of a speaking voice with the persona being one of the three men, referred to as the Magi. The persona of the poem is speaking a long time after the event has taken place and sounds as if he has been asked to tell his version of the events. The whole poem is like an allusion to the Bible or Christmas story and is typical of T. S. Eliot, as the tone is not very cheerful.

*The commentary begins with a brief summary of the content and narrative point of view of the source text, with a vague comment about it being 'an allusion to the Bible'* and a generalisation about Eliot's tone. There is no reference to the transformation or the writer's intentions.

Eliot uses post-modification throughout the poem, which is a feature of speech, especially of tired speech.

*✍ This is an unsubstantiated assertion about the nature of 'tired speech'. The commentary, so far, is a critical analysis of Eliot's poem rather than a reflection on the relationship between the two texts.*

Instead of saying 'hostile cities' he says 'cities hostile'. Other examples of this include 'towns unfriendly' and 'villages dirty'.

*✍ The candidate exemplifies post-modification here.*

This use of post-modification adds to the weary tone of the poem. The language is closer to spoken English than written English — this is emphasised by the post-modification, the repetition of the word 'journey', and the listing technique of the word 'and' (shown below):

> And running away, and wanting their liquor and women
> And the night fires going out, and the lack of shelters.

This use of 'and' becomes foregrounded heavily as a weary complaint. A semantic field of negative lexis, with words such as 'cursing', 'wet', 'darkness' and 'hostile', adds to the depressing tone of the poem. Another feature of speech is the colloquial language, for example 'we had of it'. There are also a few caesuras in the poem to add to the conversational style, such as:

> Finding the place; it was (you may say) satisfactory.

Eliot also uses deixis, for example 'these kingdoms' instead of using personal pronouns, such as 'my', which would emphasise possession. This shows that for the Magus the journey was very much psychological, as he no longer sees his kingdoms as home.

*✍ This commentary is becoming a linguistic analysis of 'The Journey of the Magi'. The candidate demonstrates a clear grasp of and accurate use of linguistic terminology (post-modification, deixis) but to what end? If you are going to give an account of the style of the original text, this must be related to your transformation. For example, have you kept or altered the style? If so, why? So far, the candidate has not mentioned the new piece at all, so has not yet written a commentary. A moderator would find this unsatisfactory.*

The lines of the poem have an unfinished feel to them because of the weak line endings. At the beginning, there is no real, strong, rhythmical pattern to the poem and the rhythm is irregular. However, towards the middle of the poem the rhythm becomes stronger. The rhythm is slow but speeds up occasionally. It becomes very broken in the last stanza, which expresses the persona's confusion. The last line is foregrounded because it is on its own and does not fit in with any of the other patterns:

> I should be glad of that.

*All that the candidate has said so far may be true, but the points made in the moderator's comment above remain valid for this section. There has been no reference to the candidate's own piece.*

The beginning of the poem starts with a quotation from Lancelot Andrewes in 1622:

> A cold coming we had of it
> Just the worst time of the year
> For a journey, and such a long journey:
> The ways deep and the weather sharp,
> The very dead of winter.

I incorporated this quotation into my transformation, which is a piece of travel writing. The idea came from the travel writings of Bill Bryson and his texts, for example *Notes from a Small Island*. I took on the format of his titles and called my piece *Notes from the Middle East*. The quote by Andrewes features in the second paragraph of my text and is used in the same context as it is in the poem, to describe the weather. However, in the poem, Eliot does not state that his first few lines are a quotation but uses them as part of the Magus's words. Whereas I used it as an actual quotation:

> It reminded me of a quotation I know of, from Lancelot Andrewes in 1622.

*This section contains the first reference to the new text. We learn of the candidate's style model and choice of title, but these comments are not especially illuminating. The candidate also describes how she has used the Lancelot Andrewes quotation, but not really why she has done so. So far, the commentary is unsatisfactory.*

The tone of my piece is upbeat, unlike that of the original, in order to bring a sense of humour in. The fictional writer Sam Weston does not understand the importance of the journey and somewhat misunderstands the whole point.

*This is a potentially illuminating point about the contrast between the two texts. It would have been better had the candidate developed this by explaining why she chose such a narrator and the effects she hoped to achieve.*

> As the Magi set back for their own kingdoms, they muttered something about a loss of identity. Surely they did not mean they had lost their passports?

Like the original, my piece is written in the first person to give an account of the entire journey to the birth of Jesus. The piece is negative in style but not in a serious way like the original poem is. The complaints throughout my piece are very minor, for example, the writer complains about the cold weather, her lack of a tan and the lack of sleep. The Magus mentions the cold and the lack of sleep in the poem but simply says 'There were times we regretted'. There are much more serious issues discussed in the original:

> But had thought they were different, this birth was
> Hard and bitter agony for us, like death, our death.

🖊 Here the candidate demonstrates an understanding of the differences in tone and approach between the two texts but, again, she would have done better to explain why she made the changes she did. However, the commentary is now more satisfactory — it is more focused on the differences between the two texts than on linguistic analysis of the original poem.

These issues in the transformation are mocked by the persona and made humorous:

🖊 Yes, but why?

Set down what exactly? The lovely warm cup of coffee I was clutching?

These complaints emphasise the difference in attitudes and values between the two pieces.

🖊 What are these differences? The candidate would have gained more marks if the commentary explored these differences rather than merely stating that they exist.

The travel piece is written in the present day, whereas the poem was supposed to be written a long time ago, which shows why attitudes are different. But the misunderstanding of Sam Weston is the main reason.

The second part of the travelogue, 'Return to the Middle East', where Sam revisits the same places 3 years later to see if the economy has altered, shows an even deeper misunderstanding. In the third paragraph, the Magus speaks of 'Alien Kingdoms', as he does in the poem, and when the narrator says 'Then it struck me', the reader expects Sam to go on and explain what the Magus means. However, she says instead, rather trivially, 'Do they have televisions in the Middle East?'

I used similar lexis to that of the original piece, such as 'camel men', 'silken girls' and 'sherbet'. However, I did not use post-modification

🖊 The candidate is attempting to link the earlier comments about post-modification with some of the stylistic changes she has made.

as this piece is supposed to be a throughout

🖊 The candidate would have benefited from proofreading her work more carefully.

piece of writing unlike the poem, which has the format of an interview.

🖊 The transformation is not actually in the format of an interview.

Another example, which shows the piece to be more similar to written English than spoken English, is the rhetorical questions that appear throughout the text:

Could it be that this journey had some sort of other purpose? I did not know. It certainly had not been a holiday. I didn't even have a tan, so what then?

The language of the piece is such that the reader becomes closer to the writer as the writer talks about how she is feeling and what she is thinking:

Now, first, I was under the impression that Israel was a hot country. Well, it wasn't.

The difference in purposes between the two pieces is quite small. The poem features in a book of poetry by T. S. Eliot and is there for entertainment purposes.

*This is a naïve and generalised comment.*

The piece of travel writing would feature in a magazine as an informative article; however, it also has a large amount of entertainment purposes. The poem is more intellectual than the article but both are for entertainment.

*These points about differences in purpose and audience are simplistic. It is appropriate that the candidate should explore such issues in a commentary as they are central to a transformation, but a better commentary would have discussed them in greater depth.*

*For example, the Eliot poem is meant to provoke our own response to the Nativity — it is not mere 'entertainment'. The candidate should have addressed issues such as whether she was trying to demonstrate the secular nature of the narrator's personality (and perhaps, by extension, the nature of the society in which she lives).*

The audiences, however, of the two pieces would not be similar at all. The reader of the poem is most likely to be an intellectual person who enjoys literature, whereas the audience of the article may be more likely to be a woman looking purely for entertainment.

The style and structure of the two pieces are also completely different. The poem is set out in three clear stanzas with a weary tone and the persona being one of the Magi. The article is a piece of text, with pictures and a humorous style. The persona is a fictional character travelling with the Magi:

My journeys this month took me to the Middle East.

*This paragraph gives simplistic comments that are more descriptive of what the candidate has done than analytical of why these changes were made.*

The other main difference between the two is the time period they are set in. The transformation is set in the present day, with reference to modern technology

I mentioned to the Magi that maybe a nice jeep or something would have been the better option…

The original poem is set a long time ago, at the birth of Jesus when society and culture were completely different. They travelled by camels as there were no other means of transport and the poem uses fairly archaic language, such as 'liquor' and 'folly'.

*'Liquor' and 'folly' are not examples of archaic language. They are in common, if formal, use today.*

The transformation almost seems to have two different time zones, with the persona living in the present day and the Magus living hundreds of years ago.

Finally, I did make some changes whilst I was transforming 'The Journey of the Magi'. My first draft seemed too much like a piece from a woman's gossip column and needed more information. I also changed the title from *Notes from a Strange Place* to *Notes from the Middle East* and added a concluding section to the article named 'Return to the Middle East'. The piece also needed to be made longer which meant that more information was vital.

*M.* This is a lost opportunity. The candidate could have explored in more depth the reasons for making particular changes — this would probably have indicated more of her intentions in writing this piece. The suspicion that the second part of the article was added mainly to increase the word count seems justified by the comments in this paragraph.

*M.* **This commentary is not as successful as the transformation it accompanies. It spends too long analysing the language of the original, without using this analysis productively. When the candidate does write about the changes she made and the decisions she reached about the new text, the comments remain superficial and descriptive. This commentary was awarded 14 marks.**